641

W9-BJJ-272

# "Gimme Rewrite, Sweetheart..."

# "Gimme Rewrite, Sweetheart..."

## Tales from the Last Glory Days of Cleveland Newspapers

*Told by the Men and Women Who Reported the News*

## John H. Tidyman

GRAY & COMPANY, PUBLISHERS
CLEVELAND

© 2009 by John H. Tidyman

All rights reserved. No part of this book may be reproduced or transmitted in any form or manner without written permission from the publisher, except in the case of brief quotations embodied in critical articles and reviews.

Gray & Company, Publishers
www.grayco.com

Library of Congress Cataloging-in-Publication Data
Tidyman, John H.
Gimme rewrite, sweetheart : tales from the last glory days of Cleveland newspapers / John Tidyman.
p. cm.
ISBN 978-1-59851-016-4
1. American newspapers—Ohio—Cleveland. 2. Reporters and reporting—Ohio—Cleveland. 3. Cleveland (Ohio)—Newspapers. I. Title.
PN4899.C63T53 2009
071.71'32—dc22
2009013871

Printed in the United States of America
10 9 8 7 6 5 4 3 2 1

*For Carl F. Rak, Ph.D.,*
*who lighted the light and said, "Let's go."*

# Contents

# Preface

Never has the end of an era been so easily and accurately determined. The newspaper era in Cleveland ended on June 17, 1982, when the staff of the *Cleveland Press* was rudely shoved out the door and sympathetic *Plain Dealer* reporters, black bands affixed to their biceps, came over to share the shock, disbelief and grief.

Cleveland was always a great town for newspapers; for much of the 20th century, the town was served by three major metropolitan dailies, the Cleveland *Plain Dealer*, the *Cleveland News* and the *Cleveland Press*. Only one remains.

Newspapers have always been a spectacular response to the freedoms guaranteed—and tested—in the First Amendment. Journalists bring to the citizenry the dark side of government, the comings and goings of good people and bad, the plans that inspire high hopes as well as details of inevitable disasters. A good newspaper is an intimate and integral part of any town; any big city without competing newspapers should be ashamed of itself.

This book is a collection of stories and memories from the reporters, editors and photographers of Cleveland's last newspaper era, which is fading away faster and faster.

In Cleveland's long and storied history there may have been worse days than June 17, 1982. Me, I don't think so.

"Well, you could'a been a plumber."

— Legendary *Cleveland Press* reporter Bus Bergen, to complaining colleagues.

# 1.

## *"Screw the competition."*

[ THE PRESS VS. THE PD ]

*When Cleveland was a two-paper town, part of every great story was beating the competition. The ongoing battle between the* Press *and the* Plain Dealer *was a visceral, no-holds-barred street fight. At the police beat, reporters from one paper would create fake stories and watch the competition race out the door. Sportswriters sought to gain the confidence of players, managers, owners, refs and umpires, batboys and trainers—anyone who could be a reliable source. Often it was ex-girlfriends of players, saloon keepers, scouts and lawyers. Competition was on the calling cards of court reporters and almost tattooed on the chests of political reporters. City desk editors kept score in their memories, managing editors expected to be first always, and colleagues toasted each other for great stories. Many considered lying to get to the truth—and get it faster than the other paper—to be a virtue.*

RUSS MUSARRA

*General Assignment Reporter,* Press

You learned your lessons the hard way. I learned how to cajole pictures from grieving wives and mothers. On the night shift, if somebody got killed in an automobile accident or a shooting or whatever, you'd want to get a picture. Michael Kelly was a reporter for the *Plain Dealer*. Well, Mike was a very nice person. He just couldn't do enough for you. He and I went out to a grieving parent's home one time to get pictures of somebody who had died. We got there at the same time and he said, "Let me do the talking." We were talking and getting information. I'm writing as fast as I could. He said, "Do you have any pictures of little Johnny?" And so she brought out the pictures of him and he took them all. He said, "Thank you so much." He's leaving, and I said, "Do you have any more pictures?" She said, "Well, no. I gave them all to him." I said, "Well, Mike." He said, "Screw you." If you got there first, take them all. Screw the competition.

JIM DUDAS
*Reporter,* Press

The competition was so fierce that I once bribed a prisoner with a carton of Lucky Strikes if he promised that, after our interview, he would not talk with the reporter for the morning paper.

MIKE ROBERTS
*Reporter, Editor,* Plain Dealer

The heyday for the *Press* was in the '40s and '50s. By the '60s, television was beginning to impact the afternoon papers. Then the *Plain Dealer* was beginning to move against the *Press*. There were a lot of young guys at the *PD*. Everybody was aggressive as hell and there was as much competition in-house as there was against the *Press*. If you had a good story on your beat you'd look over and there'd be two or three of your own guys there because they'd leave their beats and come and try to get a piece of the story. And the rule was—we had a game we played—the game was nothing mattered unless it was Page 1 above the fold. And on that night if you got that, you'd wait for the paper to come out— the early edition—you'd sit at the Headliner and have a beer, and there was no better feeling. That was really the great time for reporting, when you could score a headline and it mattered. The times were great, because the stories were there in the civil rights era and we were writing about things we could see, the riots, the marches, Rev. Bruce Klunder getting run over by the bulldozer. These were significant, important stories—the emergence of the black leaders in town; Carl Stokes was beginning to make his political run. It was a very exciting time.

WHITEY WATZMAN
*Reporter,* Plain Dealer

The atmosphere at the police station was always fraught with tension. It wasn't just the deadlines; it was the competition. To be scooped by the police reporters of the *Press* or the *News*—this was a calamity that we all dreaded. Suppose there was a fire at 10:30 P.M., with several persons burned and arson suspected—and that we *Plain Dealer* guys were unaware of it. (Not every incident was reported in detail, if at all, on the police radio.) Suppose, then, that the *Press* greeted its readers the next day with that story in large headlines on Page 1. We'd gotten scooped. The fire had broken out "on our time," which is to say in time for the morning *Plain Dealer* to report it first, but we'd missed it. The next day, we'd have to do a follow-up on a story that the morning paper should have already had. This was humiliating. We'd have to live with the self-satisfied smirk of the *Press* reporter. (Some, not all, acted that way.) Being scooped was dangerous too. Ben Tidyman would have to explain the failing to the city editor, who'd demand to know who among us had been on duty. Ben would stoutly defend us, but not always convincingly.

DICK PEERY
*Reporter,* Plain Dealer

The competition kept the adrenaline going. There was a charge in getting something that the *Press* missed, and when they beat you, it just made you go back and try harder. One of my favorite memories is of waiting a long time for the Cleveland school board to come out of executive session and start the meeting. While the *Press* reporter sat looking at the ceiling, I used the time to thumb through the voluminous agenda and saw they were hiring a laborer who had the last name of a board member. The lead on my story the next day was something like "Schools vote to cut teaching positions and hire the son of a board member." The *Press* reporter told me that I got him in big trouble because he had missed it.

BILL BARNARD
*Reporter, Editor,* Plain Dealer

One day a call came in for a traffic fatality near University Circle. Then they were calling for homicide. Then a double homicide. The victim was a senior partner at Baker Hostetler who was having an affair with a woman attorney. The woman's estranged husband was waiting for them, with a shotgun, when they came home. He shot the attorney first, who stumbled down the stairs, got into his car and died. Then the woman was shot. The wife of the victim was being taken upstairs at Central Station. Bob Tidyman walked on the elevator, interviewed her between floors and had the interview on Page 1 the next morning. It was interesting. We had a managing editor who decided it was bad style to run crime news on Page 1, so we had one column going down the right side, and inside the full story. The *Press* had a huge headline: "Give Up, Max, Father Urges," and the whole front page on the murder case.

WILLIAM F. MILLER
*Reporter,* Plain Dealer

Just before Christmas in 1967, we got a call that the Silver Bridge over the Ohio River had collapsed. The city editor came to my desk and said, "Get a plane and fly down there and cover it. Dudley Brumbach [who was an old-time photographer] is going to take the photos and another reporter, Joe Eszterhas, is going to accompany you, so get as much information as you can and get back."

I was lucky I was able to get a plane. We rented it at Burke Lakefront and we took off. Fortunately, they had a freelance pilot; first time I ever encountered that. This guy was working weekends so he flies us down there on December 15, 1967. Problem was, there wasn't, at that time, an airport. They were building one. But this young pilot said, "We're going to get you there." If we went to one in another part of the state, we'd never have time to cover the story. We were coming over the airport and you could see the construction there.

"Should we try to land there?" the pilot asked.

"Let's land," I said.

He put that plane down just beautifully and we landed on the runway, and there we found the governor's plane. "I'll pull up close to them," the pilot said

Two state troopers came at us and stopped us and said, "What are you guys doing here?" and I quickly said, "The governor wants to see us." (I'm sure he did want to see us.)

"Get in my car and we'll take you over there," the trooper said.

My God, it was luck. He took us over and put us right in the lap of the governor. Then we decided to split up, spread out, meet in an hour and start calling in. That would make deadline and beat the *Press* and everybody else. We spread out and started talking to people. This was really a tragedy and a half, I'm telling you. There were 31 cars thrown off the bridge. The bridge had crumbled. Forty-six people died. The city desk wanted me to come back with Dudley and write cutlines and give the first account. Eszterhas wanted to stay through the morning. We got back in the plane, flew to Cleveland and made the first deadline. We had it first.

HELEN MOISE
*Food Writer,* Press

The *Press* had more of a connection with the community be-cause number one with Louie Seltzer was that you answer your phone when it rings. And we did. Up until the very end, we did. And that was just the way we were brought up. The *Plain Dealer*—they would only take phone calls on certain days up to a certain hour, but we did it all the time. I would see people at fairs and I would recognize their voice from the phone calls. I'd say, "Are you so-and-so who calls all the time?" They'd say, "Yes." I'd say, "Yeah, I recognized your voice."

FRED MCGUNAGLE
*Suburban Editor, General Assignment,* Press

I got a job at the *Plain Dealer* as a copy boy in August of '55. And I spent four weeks there. And after about three weeks, I thought that maybe if this is the newspaper business, I was wrong about wanting to be in it. There were people who really didn't care very much. The only person I ever saw move very fast was the woman answering the telephone when someone called to say, "They're towing your car." So I called up Louie Clifford at the *Press.* He knew me because we had invited him out to talk to our journalism clinic at John Carroll, and he put in a word for me.

BILL TANNER
*Reporter, City Editor,* Press

With the *Press* being competitors as we were, we were always operating at top speed. We always tried to get our editorials the next day after something happened. A lot of newspapers waited one, two or three days. That doesn't mean that your comments are any good, it just means that you're quick.

When I joined the *Press*, there was what they called the "night" edition, which was really the city edition. There were two home editions, the first edition, the city edition, and two finals—the early final and the late final. They had two-star makeover, the final would be four stars, and the final-final would be five stars.

You didn't get lessons in the business then; you were self-taught. You developed your sense of news, either innately or by observing or both. The *Press*'s sense of news was probably a little different from the *Plain Dealer's*, for a lot of different reasons; one of the big reasons, of course, was the time of day. The *Plain Dealer*, being a morning paper, had a greater choice of national news because news is made overnight; therefore, they'd get the first crack at any national story.

HELEN MOISE
*Food,* Press

We competed with the *Plain Dealer*. Get that strawberry shortcake recipe out. Get it out this week. Beat them to it. It was funny. We were competitive. We had to get our biscuits or what-ever—we had to get our latkes in before they did, all those recipes that people wanted every year. They're in season, because we only wrote about things in season, which a lot of them don't do anymore. But that was how we competed—get that strawberry shortcake out.

JIM MARINO
*Criminal Courts Reporter,* Press

There was a *Plain Dealer* courthouse reporter who was my competition, a guy named Van Vliet. He just had such an ob-noxious way about him that most of the judges didn't like him. They would, right in front of him, say, "Van Vliet, we've got no stories for you today. Oh, Jim Marino, from the *Press*, come into my chambers." They'd do it right in front of Van Vliet to tick him off. So here are my bosses back at the city desk thinking that I'm beating the pants off of the *Plain Dealer* because I'm so much a better reporter than the other guy, and the truth of the matter was that the judges just disliked him.

MARGE ALGE
*Society Writer,* Press

The *Press* was a marvelous place to work. First of all, everybody was a personality and a talent, I suppose. And they were crazy.

TOM SKOCH
*General Assignment Reporter,* Press

When I was in Lake County, there was a huge murder story in Mentor that Jim Marino and I worked on, and I always thought it would make a great movie. A young man, H. Thomas Hoffman III, killed his parents for insurance money, and eventually went to prison.

It started out with a small fire. The paperboy noticed smoke curling out of a house and called the fire department. The fire department went to the house and put out a small fire. There were two people dead. So they took the two people in to the coroner, and a little while later, the coroner says, "They've got bullet holes in them." That started the whole big investigation. Their son— people always said, "He's a great guy"—ended up being a killer.

For a couple of weeks, there was a big go-around where he slowly became a suspect and he was denying the killings. At one point, he even held a news conference in the living room of his in-laws' house. All the Cleveland media showed up for this. The driveway was full of cars. One TV reporter pulled in and rear-ended some other reporter's car. That was how everyone was: in a big rush and tumble to get there.

Tommy Hoffman was sitting in the chair at one end of the room and his wife next to him and around him in a big circle

were all these reporters asking him questions. We were on deadline at the *Press*. Hoffman would answer questions, and Jim Marino would dash out in the kitchen and grab the phone and call
in the quotes to—I think Dick McLaughlin was taking the story
at the time. And Mac was typing the story and handing off the
pages to be set in type while the news conference was going on.
Marino read through his notebook and then he'd run back in the
living room.

And then I'd run into the kitchen with more quotes. So this
was a live broadcast newspaper interview. We wanted to keep
that phone line open because the *Press* was on a deadline. And
there was an older lady reporter from the *Painesville Telegraph*,
Hilda Fastman, who was their star reporter. Hilda wanted to use
the phone and I think she went for it just as I was trying to get to
the phone. I didn't want her to bust the phone connection to the
*Press* because we had to get all this stuff. So I kind of gave Hilda
a body check. I think that's the only time I ever hit a woman. I
feel bad about it. I mean, I didn't slug her. I just sort of bumped
her aside.

V. DAVID SARTIN
*Reporter,* Plain Dealer

I enjoyed the competition. Well, as a police beat reporter you
knew the *Press* came out several times in the morning and they
would sometimes, often, have the jump on a breaking story, a
midnight murder, or a 2 A.M. murder. They would often have the
jump on it, and then they had that edition that came out around
9 A.M. And then they ran several editions throughout the day,
and you knew that this story you wanted for your first edition that
night had to beat the pants off what the *Press* had done all day—
and you wanted not just to take the next development, but to get
the solid, better story to start with. The one they could not catch
up to at 9 A.M. You wanted that one. I enjoyed that a lot. I faced

the *Press* as a police reporter, a suburban reporter, as a rewrite guy and later as a beat reporter. When you had a beat where you went against a *Press* reporter, your heart would sink when they had a better story than you.

DICK PEERY
*Reporter,* Plain Dealer

The staff at the *Press* was just as good as the *Plain Dealer's*, but afternoon papers were declining and dying everywhere for reasons beyond the control of the newsrooms. But without the *Press*, it seemed *Plain Dealer* editors were more willing to hold stories or forgo them altogether.

WALLY GUENTHER
*Investigative, General Assignment Reporter,* Press

With the two newspapers, you were always trying to outdo the other—with story content and everything else. Afterwards, it was the same reporters we'd have a beer with. But breaking a news story, anytime, you're fighting each other. That was a fun time in the newspaper business in Cleveland. And I think the public was rewarded for it.

# 2.

# Stop the Presses!

[ THE BIG STORIES ]

*Getting big news to a big audience was never easy. Getting it done right and on deadline was one of the satisfactions only journalists understand. In addition to the very real concerns of getting the who-what-when-where-why-and-how of a story, a minor anxiety roiled under the surface: What does my competition know? Who are they talking to? Are my sources up to this story, can I get this and make deadline, where the hell is that photographer . . .*

*Bylines were journalism's answer to battle stars.*

*One of a newspaper's best virtues was it could tell the whole story, something radio and television couldn't do. Never did. Never will.*

JIM DUDAS

*Reporter,* Press

The year was 1971 or 1972. A federal grand jury had just handed down indictments of a number of Ohio National Guardsmen for the events on the afternoon of May 4, 1970, when the guardsmen fired upon a group of students protesting the United States' bombing of Cambodia. The guardsmen were accused of violating the civil rights of the four slain students.

I was a relatively new reporter for the *Cleveland Press.* I had just been assigned the federal courts beat. And I was hungry and aggressive.

The morning after the indictments were handed down, and reported in the morning paper, the city editor came to my desk first thing upon my reporting for work and told me to go to Wooster, a small community about two hours south of Cleveland, and see if I could talk with one of the indicted guardsmen, Matthew McManus.

None of the indicted guardsmen were answering their phones or returning calls. I had McManus' home address from the indictment. I found the home, left my car and rang the bell and rapped on the door. No answer. No surprise.

Not wanting to return empty-handed, I took a chance and found a phone booth (there were no cell phones then) and called the largest employer in town, Rubbermaid. The receptionist put me right through to McManus, a mid-level manager.

I remember to this day my exact words: "Hello, Mr. McManus, my name is Jim Dudas with the *Cleveland Press*, and I would like to get your side of the story about the indictments." I did not say shootings because it would have implied that he actually shot and/or hit a student. He was not eager to talk, but he was too polite not to.

When it appeared he was willing to talk with me, I panicked. I didn't expect the interview. I left my notebook in the car. But not wanting to slow him down or disturb him as he patiently and comprehensively answered my questions, I started writing on my hands, arms and, ultimately, my bare ankles, which, at the time, I could lift and rest on the small shelf in the booth. (Fortunately, I had only two days prior shaved my legs from the calves down in preparation for taping them for a marathon I was planning to run).

He was saying things no other guardsman had said before. He was scathing in his judgment of his commanding officers. I knew it was going to be a good story. I started running out of bare skin and he started running out of patience.

I asked if we might meet for lunch (it was then about 10 A.M.) to further explore some of his comments. "I will have to talk with my attorney," he said. "Call me back in about an hour." I knew there was not a snowball's chance in hell that his attorney would let him talk to me while under federal indictment. Still, I hung around Wooster and, while waiting, transcribed my notes from my skin to my reporter's notebook.

At precisely 11 A.M. I called McManus back. "Yes," he said, "I did talk with my attorney and he does not think it a good idea for me to talk with you." I thanked him for trying and hung up the phone. I did this hurriedly because I did not want him inquiring about what I might or might not do with the notes from our earlier conversation.

Not to be pejorative, but McManus was kind of unsophisticated, and I knew it almost immediately by the way he answered the questions. He was as unassuming and forthright as any subject I had talked with.

So here was my dilemma that I had two hours to think about as I drove back to the newspaper office. I had a great story, one we called a "one-er" (front page, above the fold). I also knew it was a national story. But I knew in my heart of hearts that McManus did not know talking to a reporter, without stipulating that it was an off-the-record conversation, could automatically be an on-the-record story.

My city editor was not expecting a story. No one else had one. McManus was not living at his home, so coming back empty-handed would not have hurt my career one bit. Only I knew I had a story. Only I knew I had a choice.

I did not want to hurt McManus. He was, after all, a fine young man, with a family, a bungalow and a comfortable existence in one of those storybook communities. And I knew a story like the one I had would cause him pain, embarrassment and, perhaps, impact the outcome of his trial.

But I had this freedom of the press thing to deal with, as well. I had my professionalism. And, yes, I had my ambition. Those three things were part of the mix, and I found it impossible to separate them.

About halfway into the ride, I forced myself to stop thinking about it. I put a Bob Seeger tape in the car stereo (I think it was an eight-track) and decided I would make a decision at the front door of the *Press*. An hour never went so quickly. There I was, facing the front door and the biggest decision of my nascent career.

Let me add that I was raised by the Golden Rule. My parents instilled fair play into all of us. There were six kids in the family and, to a kid, we all found a way to befriend those on the playground who were otherwise friendless. It was not goodness, it was just expected.

I kept putting off the decision as I slowly climbed the stairs to the building. There were 10 of them. And I took my time with each. I kept putting off the decision and decided that once I grabbed the handle of the door, I would make up my mind.

I touched the door and said to myself: "I'm going to go with it."

I ambled up to the city editor. "Bill," I said, "I think I got a hell of a story. He talked to me."

The city editor sprang into action so we could get it into that afternoon's edition. He assigned the best rewrite man on the paper (some would say one of the best in the country) to sit down with me and take my notes. I read them to him. He asked me some questions. "Are you sure he said that?" he would ask. I would look at my leg or other note-sullied skin and read my notes and reply: "Positive."

Each page was ripped from the rewrite man's typewriter and rushed to the composing room, where they were already remaking Page 1. We got it in the first edition. It was a banner headline that used the most damning quote: "We were led like blind fools." It referred to the officers.

I was the toast of the city room. That evening, gathering my stuff in preparation for going home, one of my buddies said: "You look bummed out, wanna go have a beer?" "Nah," I said, "I think I just want to go home."

That evening I got a call from Dan Rather, who, at the time was an ambitious reporter for CBS. He asked how he could contact McManus. My story had hummed across the wires and it was national news.

My feelings about McManus were swirling in my head. I knew that McManus would not likely talk to Rather. Still, I decided, in my own way, to protect the small-town kid who was suddenly thrust in the big-time spotlight.

"Dan," I said, "I can't give you that information. I have to protect my source." He understood, and hung up. At least I had that to feel good about.

MIKE ROBERTS
*Reporter, Editor,* Plain Dealer

One day a federal marshal took me aside and gave me a number on a piece of paper. He said, "Look at this case." It was a case that dealt with mobster Shondor Birns. And he was getting out of jail. In those days, to get out of jail, you had to have a job. The job that he was coming into was a vice president of Forest City Enterprises. The guy who signed him up was Sam Miller. I didn't know who Sam Miller was. I get in my car and I drive out to this office on Brookpark Road. I burst in, and the office was worse than this office—shit all over the place. I said, "Mr. Miller, Mike Roberts from the *Plain Dealer*. I want to know why you hired Shondor Birns." Sam threw me out. By the time I got downtown, he must've made some calls because when I walked in, the city editor said to me, "The next time you get something like that, talk to me before you go out there." He said, "I've been getting calls from the front office." Fast forward 40 years later and I'm in Sam Miller's office again, a much nicer office in the Terminal Tower, and I ask him about Shondor Birns and the job. "I ran numbers for him when I was a kid," Miller says. "I had to give him a job."

BILL TANNER
*Reporter, City Editor,* Press

When [John F.] Kennedy was assassinated, we put out a home makeover and a final. I was there at the time, on the desk. It was during noon hour, 1 o'clock, that he died. So he must've been shot at 12. I remember Al Prudence was on the wire desk. And it said, "Kennedy shot." He shouted it out and everybody stopped. So we immediately first made over the home edition. It caught most of our home editions, and we put out extras, and then the final.

DICK FEAGLER
*Reporter, Columnist,* Press

When Bobby Kennedy got shot, they sent me out to cover it. On the way to my hotel I stopped at the Ambassador Hotel where he was killed, and they were still cleaning up the blood. I went out and stood the death watch in the nurses' dormitory behind the hospital until I don't know what time in the morning. It was very late. It had been a long day, because whatever time it was in California, it was three hours later for me. I finally decided to go back to the hotel and get some sleep. I got about an hour's sleep. And this just goes to show you the kind of operation that Kennedy's people had. I got about an hour's sleep and the phone rang, and it was somebody on Kennedy's campaign staff calling me and telling me that he died and that we all had to be at such and such—I can't remember where—to get on the first plane at such and such a time and we'd be landing on the Marine airfield and going on to St. Patrick's Cathedral. I don't know how many reporters they had, not as many as there would be now, but there were a lot of people. And they had such a smooth operation that they could round you up, wherever you were around town. We must've had to check in and tell them where we were staying, but I thought that was kind of impressive.

WILLIAM F. MILLER
*Reporter,* Plain Dealer

There was a diesel fire on the Roger Blough, which was one of the Great Lakes ore freighters. I was dispatched—everyone was—to the Lorain shipyards to cover it. June 1971. Four workers ultimately died in the disaster. The challenge confronting reporters was how to get access to the dock area. It was a huge area. The Roger Blough was getting ready to sail. There were reporters all over the place, but they had the tightest security and reporters couldn't break it. I decided that wasn't going to work so I went over to another building nearby and wondered if I could get in that way. So I went in and there was a woman answering phones there.

"I'd like to speak to the president of your organization," I said.

"Well, sit there, because I'm really tied up," she said.

So I sat down and two people came walking out, two office workers. Here the ship was on fire and they're talking about going out for a nice lunch. I was thinking, "If these two idiots are abandoning their ship, I'm gonna get on that ship somehow."

When the receptionist wasn't looking, I just walked down the stairs. A door was open and inside a couple office workers were looking out the window at the fire. I got in back of them and stepped out on the property. I immediately started looking for a hard hat. I covered labor for years, and if you're not wearing a hard hat, it's like being with your pants off. I found one on the ground. I looked like one of the engineers, so I started finding my way to the ship. I kept my notebook hidden so I didn't look like a reporter, and I was overweight enough to look like an engineer.

I started mingling with the workers, watching the fires, and they were talking about loading the ship with fuel while working on it. I didn't say one word. I looked like an engineer with a white shirt and tie, and hard hat. Then a Salvation Army truck pulls up and a captain and a couple volunteers start taking coffee and doughnuts and loading them on the platform. Well, I started helping them. We had all these burly workers around, guys who could lift 400 pounds, and they weren't even helping. So I helped. We put the stuff on a platform that would rise. Me, the Salvation Army captain and two volunteers. So I just got on.

He lifted us right over the flames in the front of the boat and put us down in the back of the boat. We started passing out coffee and doughnuts. I copied down names that were on the back of helmets for identification. What surprised me was virtually all of the guys were smokers—and were smoking—and lots of them asking me for a light. I found out who had died and why, plenty of information. I got back on the little platform and we went over the side and down to the ground. At that time, I got into one of the offices with a telephone to call the city desk and report what I had at that point. We got the story. On site. Written in detail for the next day. Also information about the first of four who had died. Quite frankly, a pretty exciting time.

DON BEAN

*Reporter,* Plain Dealer

The worst time I ever got embarrassed was with Bill Jorgenson and Tinkerbell. Oh, yes, that hurt, because I had worked with Bill Jorgenson at the radio station, WERE, and he and I didn't get along. It's the story of Tinkerbell, the little boat that former *PD* copy editor Bob Manry sailed across the Atlantic. Manry offered the story to the *Plain Dealer*. Unfortunately, Phil Porter, who was just a wonderful executive editor, didn't think Manry would live and didn't accept his offer. What a fantastic thing that man [Manry] did. But anyway, Bill Jorgenson was working for

Channel 5 by this time with Dorothy Fuldheim and they hated each other. Oh God, they hated each other. Jorgenson went over there, and they hired a chopper and went out and found Manry in the middle of the ocean. They filmed Bob, interviewed him, and he was just outside of the harbor by this time. And there's Bill Ashbolt, the photographer, and Russ Kane, the reporter, waiting for him to land. When he landed, they handed him a *Plain Dealer* T-shirt to put on. He took the T-shirt and wrapped his garbage in it and threw it in the bay. Channel 5 offered the *Plain Dealer* the pictures and they declined them again. I just hated it that Jorgenson scooped us so much.

DICK FEAGLER

*Reporter, Columnist,* Press

I used to go places in a hurry. I'd come to work in the morning and they'd get some wild notion that I would have to cover some missing kid story in Venice, California, and they'd put me on a plane to do this, and I'd go out there and call my wife and say, "I won't be home for dinner. I'm going to Venice." And this happened very frequently then. Some of the stories I thought were a little bit of a reach, but I always wanted to go. I remember one time where they had a sniper on the roof of a building in New Orleans. So they debated a little while and decided they were going to send me to New Orleans. So I flew down there, I get into a hotel as close as possible to the location where this guy is, I check in, go up to my hotel room, I turned on the television set and they say, "Well, now, the drama has ended." I had a great night in New Orleans.

TOM SKOCH

*General Assignment Reporter,* Press

I started as an intern in June of 1969, right after school let out. The first thing that happened was the July 4, 1969, storm. It was a huge storm that devastated Northern Ohio. I was working police beat, and I remember looking out at the clouds and the terrible rain. As I'm doing police checks, first there was a death. A tree fell on somebody. Then another, and another. And pretty soon I had seven dead people and chaos outside. So I thought, "Uh-oh, time to call for the cavalry." I called Bill Tanner at home. He called out the big guns. I went out with one of the photographers going around the Edgewater Yacht Club. There were boats tossed all over the place. It was terrible. A real scary experience. There were a bunch of trees that fell down in Lakewood Park and crushed people. I think the death toll across the whole lakefront area was seven, if I remember right.

Later that summer I was doing rounds and I called the fire department and said, "What's going on?" And the dispatcher laughingly told me that the river caught on fire. I said, "What are you talking about?" He said, "An oil slick going down the river or something like that and it caught a railroad trestle on fire." So I wrote this little police brief thing and sent it in with the other stuff. When they read it at the city desk in the morning, holy shit! Betty Klaric was our environmental writer at the time—I think one of the first in the country. They realized what they had, and that became the burning Cuyahoga River story—"Shame of the Nation." It all started with a police beat call. In later years when I worked with reporters as an editor, I'd tell them, "You never know what you're going to get on this police round, so pay attention."

WALLY GUENTHER

*Investigative, General Assignment Reporter,* Press

There was the Santa Line Slaying in 1971 at Higbee's. A black man and a white man got into a dispute while they were waiting in line with their kids to see Santa Claus and the black guy killed the white guy. The guy that was killed was Jack Fitzpatrick. I went out in the afternoon to interview the family. And I got the wife and the kids to do a feature for the next day's paper. It was past that day's deadline at the *Press*. So I came back—you've got to remember at that time, in that era, racial tensions were high in Cleveland—and wrote it.

The next day they had the great idea of trying to get the killer's family interviewed, which was fine. Out I went to 96th and St. Clair. There was a photographer with me, Herman Seid. It was tense out there—now this neighborhood is all black and the victim was white and Irish. And in the *Press* final edition, I think our story said something about how he was captured in handcuffs from his mother's home. I guess he wasn't handcuffed, and they were all up in arms. So when I introduced myself on the porch where the mother is, she starts yelling. People from all over come and they're yelling. Herman takes off, goes in the car and locks the doors. And I'm yelling. I wanted to get them to tell me the story, to get his side of the story. So I'm yelling back at them. And people are hanging out windows and yelling. It was getting a little fierce.

I said, "I wasn't involved in that story yesterday. But tell me your story. Tell me about it."

I'm trying to find his wife. This went on for, I swear, a half hour. And I was standing up to them. They were going at it. Finally they said, "She's next door." I said, "I want to talk to her. I want her story. I want her side of the story." They finally marched me over there, so to speak. And the wife came down and sat in the stairway and told me their side of the story. So at least I had two sides of the story. Plus this guy had been injured in an industrial accident, I think, and there were all kinds of complications. I coaxed Herman out of the car and got a picture.

I got back to the *Press*—it must've been 10:00 or 10:30 A.M. I'm kind of shook, I want to get all of this out on paper—and the managing editor's asking, "What did they say? What did they say?" I finally told him, "Get away from me. Let me write it."

They did both stories in the home edition, the two sides. And my byline was over both of them. But I'll tell you, when I walked out of the office that day, I could've gone for a good cold beer. It was a challenge. I wasn't going to leave until they gave me their story. I kept saying, "Don't yell at me. If you want your story told, I'm the guy." I was called everything you could think of.

TONY NATALE
*Investigative, General Assignment Reporter,* Press

You know, it's funny, but whenever I covered an emotional story, I was always—this was my approach to it—I was always totally neutral. I had no emotion. I had no feeling. I was looking for facts. Because looking back over the years, whenever I got emotionally involved with a story, I got in trouble. Afterwards, of course, I might feel emotional. But when I covered a riot or any-thing that was very dramatic, in order to survive the scene, I just had to forget me. That's the best way I can describe it. So, what did I think about it? I thought it was natural. I thought this was just human beings being human beings. Afterward, I thought it was rotten, when I reflected on what they were doing and why. But I couldn't get politically involved.

RUSS MUSARRA
*General Assignment Reporter,* Press

Norman Mlachak was one of the nicest human beings. He didn't have a mean bone in his body. He was an excellent re-porter. He covered city hall and I covered housing and urban development at the same time he was covering city hall, so we were both at city hall a lot together. He was on the Beverly Jarosz case from day one. It was one of those things—early in the morn-ing, you've got a breaking story. They would send you out, even if you had a beat, if you covered some other beat, if you're the first guy in and they need a reporter, they send you out. And so Norman got the job and he stayed with it for the duration. He practically lived at the Garfield Heights police station. And I got assigned because they had more than one person working on it then. He and I ended up working a lot of stuff together on it. And it was so interesting watching his take on that story. He was just devastated by what happened to this girl. It was almost like it was family to him.

TOM SKOCH
*General Assignment Reporter,* Press

There was a guy named Ashby Leach who took over the Chessie System offices in the top of the Terminal Tower and held about 12 people hostage over some grievance he had with the Chessie System. That was a big stir. Here it is, downtown Cleveland, a business day, and all of a sudden the police called and said, "There's some guy holding a bunch of people with a shotgun in the top of the Terminal Tower, holding them hostage." The editors sent me over there, and I arrived at the base of the Terminal Tower at the same time that the first cop got there. We just sort of looked at one another. A huge crowd had gathered, and all kinds of police reporters and reporters from everywhere. They wouldn't let us up, obviously, but there was this one cop who was sort of like a Groucho Marx character, and he was trying to keep order. And he was so funny. I ended up writing a sidebar story just about him and how he kept everybody at bay, because everybody was trying to get up into the Tower and asking a million questions. At one point he said, "If God were to smack me off my horse and make me a lieutenant right now, I'd let you go up there, but I'm only a sergeant."

BARBARA WEISS
*Reporter,* Press

The takeover of Terminal Tower . . . I was working police beat that morning, and the news came over, I think, the scanner, or somebody called us from the city desk, and they wanted us to start calling in to the Terminal Tower. We had those Haines directories at that time where you could tell who was in the building.

So I started calling around, "Do you know what's going on there? Do you know what floor it's on?" I'm running into a brick wall.

Finally, I get this gal who says, "Well, I don't really know, but my friend works up there and I'm pretty sure it's her office."

"What's the number?"

She gives me the number and I call. I said, "I understand that there's a problem up there somewhere on that floor? I understand hostages have been taken."

She said, "Yeah."

Then I said, "Are you one of them?"

She said, "Yeah."

And I didn't get much more. I don't even remember what else after that. She was made to hang up. But talk about luck. I don't think I got her name because all of the sudden she said, "I have to hang up." But at least we knew for sure that that was the phone number. That's what kept the adrenaline going—when you hit something like that.

STUART ABBEY

*Reporter, Copy Editor, Editor,* Plain Dealer

When Forest City Publishing owned the *Plain Dealer*, it also owned a radio station, and a radio reporter would stop in to see what was going on. One time, a *PD* police reporter was on the phone, yelling for the benefit of the radio guy, "What? A boat rammed Captain Frank's? And Captain Frank's is sinking?" The radio guy pulled on his helmet, jumped on his scooter and was gone. We heard on the radio, "News Flash: Captain Frank's Restaurant, on the end of the East Ninth Street pier, has been rammed by a boat and is sinking."

JIM MARINO
*Criminal Courts Reporter,* Press

There was a case called "Little Arthur Noske," where a mother reported her kid had walked away from her at Parmatown shopping center. The truth of the matter was her boyfriend, a Brecksville doctor, had killed her son, he claims, by accident. He got mad at the kid because the kid didn't know his homework assignment for the next day. So as it came out in court, he pushed the kid, the kid bounced off the corner of the table in the bathroom, hitting his temple, and the kid was dead. So he tries to burn the kid in the fireplace in their Brecksville home while the mother watched. There was all this gruesome testimony I had to cover. The doctor realized he was headed for a conviction so he took a plea. They sent him to prison, and shortly after he went to prison Dr. Stewart Cutler died of pneumonia. End of story. But that was a front pager for weeks on end and I covered every aspect of it. That's when I realized—I can't really call it fun, but I can certainly call it interesting to be in on covering a story that you know every household in Cleveland is reading that night.

BILL TANNER
*Reporter, City Editor,* Press

I covered the Sheppard story along with a lot of other people. It was a very competitive story. My first assignment was to talk to Sam Sheppard, and I did. I got to see a lot of Sam. He actually let me talk to him up until he was indicted. I was able to have access to Richard and Steve and Sam, and I printed their side. I gave their protests and their bitching about the coverage. I did what every good reporter does, I pretended to be sympathetic, and nobody else was. This was one of the great duplicitous things about the business—the best reporters win the confidence of people and then betray them. Betrayal is probably too strong a word, but you ingratiate yourself for the purpose of getting information. And then you uningratiate yourself by printing what you think is the truth.

DICK FEAGLER

*Reporter, Columnist,* Press

I nearly got blitzed in the cafeteria one day because of the Sam Sheppard case. I covered a little bit of the second trial. I didn't get the juicy part. They'd send me over in the afternoon to cover it in the final edition. I remember going in the cafeteria one day and the subject of Sam came up. And I said—rather mildly, I thought—"Well, I'm not saying he didn't do it, but I don't think they ever had the evidence to pin it on him." And whoa, they were going to throw me out of the building. The paper was so hot to trot on that story. But that, by the way, is still my opinion. I think he did it, but I don't think they ever had the evidence to pin it on him. And I guess the second trial kind of backed me up on that one.

DAVID SARTIN

*Reporter,* Plain Dealer

Sam Sheppard? I don't know. I met a large number of old timers, particularly cops, who believed he did it. A bit of irony: in my days in the '60s, in journalism school, the Cleveland newspapers were held up as an example of what you did not do as a reporter in a crime story.

# 3.

# "There's a report of a dead body . . ."

[ THE POLICE BEAT ]

*For most reporters, the police beat is where it all began. Cleveland police headquarters were at East 21st Street and Payne Avenue. Just a well-thrown snowball north were the Cuyahoga County jail and common pleas courts. Police and fire news were important beats at all the newspapers. Not only was the news important, but the police beat served as a training ground for new reporters.*

*The chief police reporter was responsible for scheduling three shifts as well as teaching new reporters the difference between journalism class and real life. It was here new reporters met criminals and prosecutors, fire chiefs and fire victims, Payne Avenue saloonkeepers, the flotsam and jetsam of city life.*

*The pressroom in police headquarters consisted of three small rooms on the first floor. One each for the* Cleveland Press, *the* Cleveland News *and the* Plain Dealer. *Each room had mismatched chairs, a couple desks and a jumble of telephones, a couple battered Royal or Underwood typewriters, stacks of triple-carbon copy paper and ashtrays. The floors were dirty enough that the five-second rule was repealed. Those rooms were the front-line command post, but there was also fun to be had there. Poker was played, whiskey and beer were consumed, cigars and cigarettes smoked, illicit sex enjoyed and lots and lots of books read.*

WHITEY WATZMAN
*Reporter,* Plain Dealer

It was perfectly natural to come clambering into the police station through that large rear window in the *Plain Dealer* pressroom. Lots of Damon Runyon-esque characters around town did that, including shysters acting as defense lawyers, prosecutors hungering for judgeships, bail bondsmen who dreaded that their clients might become fugitives, policemen and detectives hurrying to the roll call, and, now and then again, habitual defendants who knew their way around the building and were reporting again for a preliminary hearing. For them, the window was a shortcut that had them trampling over my desk, which I shared with another police reporter or two, depending on who among us five was working at that time. The desk was flush with the windowsill, so our visitors had no choice but to slam their heels on it.

WHITEY WATZMAN
*Reporter,* Plain Dealer

I don't know, since it was so difficult to get a word out of Ben Tidyman, how well he really did playing the horses. But I do know how masterful he was as a newspaperman. Inert like a crocodile, he'd lunge suddenly when a major story broke, opening jaws so large that they'd swallow almost whole all the information that was needed to report the story completely. I recall him taking charge when a 9-year-old girl was molested and murdered near her home, after her parents had sent her to the store. A man who didn't give his name telephoned us (within a quarter hour of the discovery of the body, as it turned out) and asked for Ben. Annoyed, Tidyman arose and took the chair at the phone, which I yielded to him. We didn't know then that the caller was a detective lieutenant at the scene, tipping off Tidyman that an atrocious crime had been committed. Detectives never called us—only

Ben. We had to scratch to find out what was going on. If we did get a tip and were able to get through to whoever was in charge, that office would be tight-lipped. We'd get the "no comment" treatment. In this case, had Ben not been on hand to receive the phone call it might have been an hour or so before the rest of us learned from formal channels—too late for first edition—that a child's life had been taken.

It was about 8:50 P.M. when the call came in, and the first-edition deadline was at 9:25. Ben had to act fast but he didn't. He was deliberate. We heard only his end of the telephone conversation.

"Spell that name [the victim's] again," he said.

Then: "I'm reading it back to you."

He did, one letter at a time.

"Now tell me what happened," he said.

The rest of what we heard was a "yeah" every now and then as Ben took notes. They seemed inadequate to me. During a conversation that lasted seven or eight minutes, he jotted down perhaps a couple dozen words, one at a time, with a few symbols that evidently served as mnemonics for him. He was as stingy with words in his note-taking as he was in conversation. This was to his advantage because the slate he chose to write on—the inside cover of a cardboard matchbook—afforded him insufficient space to be expansive. It wasn't clear to me why he wasn't making use of the stack of letter-size paper at his elbow.

By 9 P.M. Tidyman had most of the story from this single news source. He phoned jumpy city editor Collins to alert him. He spent the next few moments trying to calm Collins, assuring him that he knew all about the deadline, including the fact that it was 9:25 P.M. and that a story had yet to be written. He said he'd call back in plenty of time. His next phone call was to the county morgue. The body had arrived, and Ben had some questions for the attendant. He double-checked the spelling of the

victim's name, as well as her address, with this person. He then
telephoned someone upstairs in the police station, carefully re-
counting all that he'd been told. "Is this what you've got, too?" he
asked. In the meantime, he refused to accept a frantic phone call
from Mr. Collins. "What else do you know?" Ben asked. He wrote
something else on the matchbook cover. We heard him say:

"Who did it?"

And: "Why don't you know?"

And: "Nobody saw it?"

And: "Nobody you can rely on? Okay."

Then: "Yeah."

At 9:10 P.M. he called Collins again, soothing him. "Here's the
story," he said. The city editor could afford the time to listen only
because he knew that Ben would be laconic. He switched him to
a rewrite man, who would have to write the story quickly from
facts supplied by Ben. It then became apparent, as they spoke,
that Tidyman lacked confidence in the rewrite man. So he proceeded to dictate phrases to him, in effect writing much of the
story himself. I noted that each mnemonic on the matchbook
cover was worth a sentence or two. At this point, even Ben was
speaking rapidly. He finished about 9:20 P.M., in time for the midnight edition. The story was at the top of the front page, some 15
paragraphs packed with detail. Every fact provided later proved
to be correct.

Here, then, was a man to emulate.

MIKE ROBERTS

*Reporter, Editor,* Plain Dealer

I worked for Bob Tidyman on the police beat for about six
months. Nobody really trained you in those days. Either you got
it or you didn't. And if you didn't, Tidyman would chew your
ass out. And if he chewed your ass out constantly your career
would be in the business department or the obituary desk. You
learned how to just go and do it—go after stories. And of course

on the police beat, you're faced with all kinds of situations that as a human being you've never experienced. You're not up for asking a woman who just lost her husband and two kids in an auto accident for their pictures or barging in on their home. So that became a really important aspect of developing as a reporter, because you had to abandon that sense of dignity in certain situations. And Tidyman was tough. There wasn't any hand holding. You just had to get in there and do it.

BILL BARNARD

*Reporter, Editor,* Plain Dealer

Bob Tidyman would come in around 6 P.M., call home to check on his kids, then give us a number where he could be reached and leave. If something happened, we were to first call Tidyman, who could then call Jim Collins at city desk and say something like "double homicide in Bratenahl and I've got guys covering it." He'd come rushing back, but he wanted to call it in first.

DON BEAN

*Reporter,* Plain Dealer

A typical shift would start around 6 P.M., and we'd work until 2 A.M. and grab lunch on the fly or eat it when we could. Bob Tidyman was the chief police reporter, and he would make out the schedule and he had about six or seven reporters. I'd be there when he was making out this schedule. He'd start typing, then he'd grab the paper and rip it out. He'd say, "I can't work with that s.o.b." Then he'd throw it away. Then he'd start again and take it out and say, "I can't work with that s.o.b." I'd say, "What do you say about me when I'm not here?"

DON BEAN

*Reporter,* Plain Dealer

I have to tell you about Steve Landesman. He was a Greek scholar. He later went on to be a professor of Greek at Ohio State

University, I do believe. But he'd work days so he could study. He'd take all the phones off the hook so he appeared to be busy as hell. When he started working nights, one night there was a big fire in the Flats. A huge fire down there, one of those warehouses. It was a very cold night. Landesman called Bob Tidyman, who was chief police reporter. Every time the phone rang, Tidyman would answer.

The first time Landesman called and said, "Bob, this is a huge fire down there. Can you send me some help?"

"How many fires do you have down there?" Tidyman asked

"One," Landesman said.

"Well, you can cover it."

Landesman called back and said, "Bob, it's cold down here. Can you send down some coffee?"

"Oh, the Red Cross will be there pretty soon," Tidyman said and hung up on him.

Then Landesman called again and he said, "Bob, I've got some boots in my car."

He had driven the police beat car at the scene. "Will you send somebody down with my boots?"

"Why did you have the boots in the trunk of your car?" Tidyman said.

"Well, in case I had to cover a fire and get in the water," Landesman replied.

"You should've taken them with you," Tidyman said.

He didn't care much for Landesman.

BILL BARNARD
*Reporter, Editor,* Plain Dealer

During days at the police beat you had to make rounds—the detective bureau and homicide—and see what was happening. One of the homicide detectives, Bill Kaiser, gave me a hard time and was physically threatening. Bob Tidyman heard about it, not from me, but from somebody. He went up there and threatened to kick the shit out of the guy. No one was going to mess around with his reporters.

FRED MCGUNAGLE
*Suburban Editor, General Assignment,* Press

I hadn't been working nights very long at all when there was a policeman killed on, I think, Washington Avenue and I remember going to Lutheran Hospital, and they put his body on a gurney with a sheet over it, but his shoes were sticking out and you could see the black shoes. And it made an impression on me, I guess, because I still remember it.

V. DAVID SARTIN
*Reporter,* Plain Dealer

Police reporter. I hated it. I did it about one year, and I did everything I could to get out of it because you were surrounding yourself with the grimmest aspects of life. I did it because I had to. But you learned stuff there. Don Bean was the chief police reporter, and he knew where the cold beer was and the good sandwiches. Another one was Harry Christiansen at the *News.* I told him the story about how I learned that you had to leave the house with a pocketful of dimes, and he told me when he was young he had to leave the house with a pocketful of nickels because that was streetcar fare. You would go up to the city desk and get an assignment and there would be a cigar box at the city desk full of nickels. You took a handful because you knew they were sending you somewhere.

JIM MARINO
*Criminal Courts Reporter,* Press

I joined the *Press* through the college placement office at Bowling Green State University. That was in 1970. I majored in journalism. I was the editor of the college paper, the *BG News*. I was hired as a summer intern and then after I graduated, they started me on police beat working days until they thought they could trust me. Then they put me on the night shift. I learned so much on the police beat. I was one of these suburban, protected kids who didn't know that much about life, and then all of a sudden, you're thrust into the middle of a big major city with all kinds of crime and corruption and action that I only saw before on television. Here I was being thrown right into the middle of it and being asked to cover it. It was the first time I ever saw people drawing guns in anger, the first time I saw the results of traffic accidents up close and actually watched cops cover bodies with plastic cloths. I mean, all of that was new to me. I was 21 years old. What did I know?

BRENT LARKIN

*Politics,* Press

My first assignment was at the police beat for six months. I wasn't there a month, maybe two, and I got a call. I worked the 3 to midnight shift and I got a call saying there'd been an explosion at the Shaker Heights police station. The building was gone by the time I got there. It was gone. Some nut had blown it up. Only a few people died, I think. Talk about baptism by fire.

ZINA VISHNEVSKY

*Reporter,* Plain Dealer

Cleveland police officer Emil Cielec and I met at an accident scene that was also a shooting scene. For decades, he was in the accident investigation unit. He noticed I walked funny. "Do you have MS? Because my daughter does." That started a longtime friendship in which I coaxed his daughter into taking the weekly injection that has kept me walking, albeit kinda funny, for nearly 20 years. From the day I met Emil, I had no trouble at crime scenes. Cops would let me into their cars to warm up, chauffeur me around during their investigations and treat me like a sister.

MIKE ROBERTS
*Reporter, Editor,* Plain Dealer

The relationship between the police beat reporters and the police—it was up and down. If we wrote a story critical of the police, your car would be ticketed, they wouldn't talk to you. You'd go up to SID and try to get a picture and they'd tell you to get lost; the homicide guys would slam the door in your face. You really had to work on developing contacts there.

WHITEY WATZMAN
*Reporter,* Plain Dealer

The most loudmouthed yenta, or gossip, who kept no confidences, was an inanimate object. It was the police radio. It chattered on endlessly, its voice coming from a speaker on a shelf above and behind us. This was tiresome talk, but we had to be sure to listen to it. It kept us in touch with what was going on out on the street. We'd hear the dispatcher assign squad cars to the scene of an armed robbery, a mugging, a fatal traffic accident. The dispatchers had their way of warning policemen what to expect. "Car 432, you got your nose tweezers with you? There's a report of a dead body in the home at 14700 Bartlett Avenue. A neighbor says it's been there for five days." "Car 641, make that payment on your life insurance policy and hurry over to the corner of St. Clair and 141st Street. There's a man in a saloon waving a gun." "Car 31, go help a drunk who's in the street directing traffic at the corner of 40th and Payne Avenue."

TOM SKOCH
*General Assignment Reporter,* Press

There was an old lady who was killed in sort of a fleabag apartment on the near East Side, and I went there to cover it, being a police reporter. And I walked in the building and started walking up the steps toward where the apartment was, and Ralph Joyce, the homicide chief, was coming down the stairs. And I said, "Hi." He said, "Hi" to me. I just kept on going, and partway up the stairs, another policeman tried to stop me.

And I thought to myself, "Well, Joyce didn't tell me to get lost." So I told the cop, "The lieutenant says it's okay."

I kept going and I went in the room with the detectives. The little old lady is lying dead on the floor there. I was walking around looking for clues. I think she had been smothered with a pillow and killed for her Social Security money or something like that. I thought she was a little old black lady. She was a little old white lady who'd been dead in this hot apartment for way too long and had turned sort of a coffee bean color.

WALLY GUENTHER
*Investigative, General Assignment Reporter,* Press

Donna Adkins was a seven-year-old girl who was kidnapped in 1965. She was picked up and taken to a motel out in Strongsville and the guy took pictures of her, and then he shot her in the eye with a pellet gun, and dumped her near the turnpike. Some truckers picked her up. She lived. The *Press* started a fund for her that reached well above $15,000 in donations. She came from a low-income family on the West Side. And the city of Cleveland opened their hearts to the gal and sent checks in. The fund built up. Louie Seltzer, I think, was the trustee of the fund, or maybe the city editor, Louie Clifford. On the Donna Adkins case, I remember, they finally arrested the guy. They took him to jail. He came from South Euclid. I remember going to the home, on my way home. I stopped in at night to talk to the mother and get a photograph of this guy, which we didn't have. She wouldn't let me in the door. I don't know if she would tell you this or not, but

I was polite to her. And I told her we had a picture of him, but it had numbers on it. She flipped open the door and she said, "That's my son's picture up there." And then she began talking. And then she gave me the photograph. Unfortunately, the guy hung himself in jail a couple of days later.

BARBARA WEISS

*Reporter,* Press

The music group Chicago came into town to play—they were arrested and then let go. I think they had some marijuana. So it was a big story, all the commotion out at Hopkins and stuff. I had gone camping over the weekend, and went directly to the police beat when I got home. I was working 4 P.M. to midnight. I get a call from Bill Tanner, who wants me to go out to somehow interview Chicago.

"I don't have any money," I said. "I don't have anything."

"Oh, you'll work something out," he said.

I was just furious. How am I going to do this? And I couldn't care less about Chicago. But I went out there, and somehow I talked my way into interviewing them during intermission. They weren't exactly the most articulate people, so it was not a great interview.

I come back, and in those days, when the *Plain Dealer* ended its shift, a group of us from the police beat would go out and have a few beers at the 2300 Club or Shai's. We came back late and I still had to write this Chicago story. When we came back to the police beat, we brought a six-pack with us, and enjoyed it in the *PD* room.

They decided that they're going home and I thought, "Fine. I still have to write my story." So I go into my room, and I don't have my purse with my notebook with the notes. It's locked in the *Plain Dealer* room. I raced out to see who I could find, and I caught Tom Gaumer. I explained the situation, and he comes back with me and we're trying to get into there. He didn't have a key. And we're trying with credit cards and everything.

We went over to the 3rd District and the cops were making hoagie sandwiches. One of them, the cop with the big knife, comes over to see if he can help out. He breaks the knife blade in the door and then he broke the handle off it.

"Can't you shoot the lock off like they do in the movies?" I asked.

He gave me such a disgusted look and turned right around and said, "You're on your own."

So there I am, I'm frantic and I'm thinking, "What am I going to do?" Well, the transom was open. Gaumer said, "Well, let's get a broom or a mop out of the janitor closet and then you stand on my shoulders and maybe with the broom handle you can reach down, and if your purse is on the desk or anywhere near, you can maybe bring it up."

I knew I had left it on the desk right by the door. So I thought, "Well, it's worth a chance." So I got up on his shoulders with an old ratty mop. I hated to touch it. And I'm fishing. And I managed to get it under the shoulder strap and I did bring it up. Hurray for me! So that was another close call for me, but I saved myself again.

The next day I came in again, and Judy Sammon was on police beat for the *PD*. I'm coming around the corner to go to our room and she's running out of her room.

"What happened, Judy? What's going on?" I asked.

"Oh, nothing you'd be interested in," she said,

"Well, you're sure in a hurry," I said.

"I'm going to 3rd District," she said. "I want to report something. Come with me."

I went with her and she's pointing to the knife that had broken. She said, "Look at that. Somebody tried to break into our room and I'm going to make a report."

I had to tell her what happened.

WHITEY WATZMAN
*Reporter,* Plain Dealer

I found a lulu one night under the unpromising heading of "Property Lost." What caught my attention was the
amount—$5,000 in cash. The terse report, skimpy on detail,
identified the man reporting the loss and where he lost it—that's
all. It was at Hotel Cleveland on Public Square. It said no more.
I called the hotel switchboard and asked whether that man was
a registered guest. Then I asked to be connected to his room on
the fifth floor. The phone rang there—no answer. I called the
manager of the hotel, who said he knew nothing. Then I made
a series of phone calls and finally reached the policeman who'd
turned in the report.

"Sure," he said. "Some screwy case!"

"What happened?" I asked.

"You won't believe this. This here guy is a salesman from out
of town, and he collects payments, I mean in cash, for what he's
sold on the installment plan. He carries this cash around with
him. So when he checks into the Cleveland, he gets undressed
and he empties his pockets. Where does he put this stuff? On the
windowsill! He doesn't take notice that the window's half open.
He goes to the bathroom. When he comes out, the first thing he
sees is that his pile of cash has gotten smaller. He looks out the
window, there's a soft breeze blowing outside. Wafting through
it is his cash. The bills are floating like butterflies, coming down
gently on Public Square, and people walking by are amazed. The
salesman is watching when one bill comes fluttering down right
in front of the eyes of one pedestrian. It catches him on the bridge
of his nose. The man looks like he can't believe it. He looks at the
bill, puts it in his pocket and hurries off. Meanwhile, everybody
else is picking up bills off the ground and stuffing them in their
pockets. It's like pennies from heaven, but they aren't pennies—
they're 10- and 20-dollar bills. So the guy calls the police. I figure
it's for his insurance."

"Who is he? Do you know?"

"No, he's got an out-of-town address. Maybe he's a gambler or something like that—I don't know. All I know is that he's not guilty of anything on my beat. Too much to keep in a wallet, he tells me. So I ask him why not a money clip, and do you know what he says? He says that would make the wad heavier when he's carrying it around."

"Do you believe him?"

"Yeah, I figure he's on the up and up, or else he wouldn't be making a report to the police. Too bad you weren't there with a photographer!"

I phoned in the story to a rewrite man, who wrote four sparkling paragraphs for the front page.

We couldn't check out every report in the record room. Far too many of them! But we had to be alert. For example, what at first glance might seem like an ordinary case of vandalism could end up being portentous if we were sharp enough to note that it had occurred at the home of a politician. Or how about a ranking police officer? Was someone getting back at him and, if so, for what? You wouldn't immediately know, of course, but even if it were a routine case, it could be of citywide interest if the victim was a prominent person. So you had to be familiar with such names.

For example, when I called the rounds one afternoon, a policeman in fashionable Shaker Heights said, with what sounded like a yawn, "All we've had is a couple of burglaries."

I was about to say OK and hang up, but this thought crossed my mind: "Why's he even bothering to mention it?"

So I asked: "Whose house?"

The policeman toyed with me. "Nobody you'd know," he said. "Some guy named Story."

"Frank Story?" I asked, uttering the name of Cleveland's police chief.

"Yeah."

"Whose was the other house?"

"Babe Triscaro's."

I knew that name, of course.

They both lived on Lomond Boulevard—the lawman and one of his occasional targets. The same burglar struck at both places, among others on the long street. No other connection between these two burglaries, but the irony of it made a nice little news story—both the hunter and the hunted had fallen to a third party.

DON BEAN

*Reporter,* Plain Dealer

When things got slow at the police beat, it was a dangerous time for me. I got bored and kept wondering about "what if" stories.

In October of 1968, the marijuana craze was sweeping the country. So I thought, wouldn't it be wonderful if there was a modern-day Johnny Appleseed, a guy by the name of Johnny Pot, who went around the countryside planting marijuana seeds for his hippie friends? He'd leave them maps of his plantings and let them know when harvest was, and in exchange they'd give him a place to sleep and food and the drug of his choice. So I gave him a derby hat, a madras jacket, yellow sandals, and I wrote a story about federal agents chasing him from Maine to Texas.

I left the story, and that night when I laid my head to pillow, I thought, "They could fire me." That kept me up for about 10 seconds. Russ Kane was city editor then and he called me the next day and said, "This story sounds like a three-martini lunch."

I said it wasn't, and it ran—not only here, but in papers across the country. I don't usually make up stories, but this was a good one. The agent in charge of drug enforcement called me and said, "Where did you get your information?" and I said, "I don't have to reveal my sources.

"You're damn right you don't have to reveal your sources," he said. "You don't have any sources."

The great goddess of journalism has a sense of humor, and two days later there was a big marijuana bust at the airport and I covered it. They had bales and bales of marijuana. I walked up to the agent in charge and he said, "So you're Bean. If you'd been here yesterday, I would have shot you."

He said he got all kinds of calls, including one from a Hollywood agent who wanted the rap sheets on Johnny Pot because he wanted to make a movie about it. I said, "You're going to have to give me credit and a share of the profits because I made it all up."

The following April 1, I wrote another story. I said a Medina farmer, Loo Flirpa (which was April Fool spelled backward), spotted Johnny Pot planting and he called the police, and they were hot on his trail. The AP started to move on it, but someone called and said, "You'd better be careful. Bean is known to make up stories." So that one didn't get in the paper.

JIM NAUGHTON
*Reporter,* Plain Dealer

Don Bean became my mentor on the police beat, especially in the conduct of pranks. One night we were sitting there without much to do between calling rounds, and I asked Bean what we could do on such a slow night. We concocted a scheme to call the *Cleveland Press* reporter who was in the old Central Police Station in an office near ours. I think it was John Hernandes, but don't trust my memory. We found an address on Kirby Avenue in the Bratenahl area, from which we imagined you could see the Shoreway. Bean got on the phone to a household on that street. I called through the *PD* switchboard to the *Press* switchboard and down to Hernandes and pretended to be the guy Bean was keeping occupied on the phone.

I told Hernandes that I had just seen a plane land on Memorial Shoreway. What kind, he asked, and I said I wasn't sure but it looked like a four-engine job. He hung up. We knew he would saunter into our room to see if we were onto the story. This was in the era when Dick Conway was a copy kid and hung around the cop shop with his camera hoping for the big story. So when Hernandes came into our room Bean was still on the phone, I was pretending to be talking with Bratenahl police and Conway was excitedly getting his gear all set up.

Then Conway jumped out our window onto the parking ramp and got in the *PD* police beat car and revved it. Hernandes jumped into his car and tore off toward the scene. Well, Conway came back in and we had figured we'd let Hernandes get partway there and then phone him on the newfangled phone in his *Press* car and tell him we'd found out it was a hoax.

It turned out he was so eager to beat us there he did not take the time to use the key that unlocked the phone—which by then was dangling with the other keys from his car's ignition—so we couldn't reach him. As time elapsed, we figured he'd cruise around and come back. Then we heard a call on police radio that, as I recall, was like this: "This is car 596. We've got a *Press* reporter who says there's a plane down on the Shoreway."

All hell broke loose. Sirens everywhere. Coast Guard checking the Lake Erie shore. Police driving over Bratenahl golf course. We lived in fear for months that we'd be found out, but so far as I know neither the authorities nor Hernandes ever traced it to Bean and Conway and me.

DON BEAN

*Reporter,* Plain Dealer

Judy Sammon was a beautiful blond woman. She was the first woman assigned to the police beat. I was the chief police reporter, and I had day fantasies and night fantasies and daydreams and night dreams about her and me working together. She had a rich boyfriend who would come down and wait for her to get off work at 11 P.M. He always wanted to go out on a big story with her.

One night she went to the Minute Chef for dinner and I called her and said, "The mother of the unknown soldier is going to put flowers on her son's grave at the Soldiers and Sailors Monument."

"Do we cover this every year?" she asked.

"No, we haven't covered this story in a long time," I said.

Her boyfriend was ecstatic. Off they went to Public Square and asked a cop, "Where's the tomb of the unknown soldier?"

He said, "Beats the hell out of me."

Then they asked a cabbie, who told them it was in Washington, D.C. She called and said, "Don, how long do I have to wait for this woman?"

"How long must you wait for the mother of the *unknown* soldier?"

Pause.

"Oh, you bastard, Bean! You bastard!"

I had to recount this reportorial adventure in the city room and when she walked in the next day, she got a standing ovation.

BARBARA WEISS
*Reporter,* Press

I worked the 4 to 1 shift on the police beat. I met some friends down in the Flats. I think it was a Friday night. We were having a good time down at Shooters, and we lost track of time, and I never bothered to check in with the morgue, because you know how you used to have to make all those calls. So I go back, finally, late to the police beat room.

When I walked in I said to John Coyne, who was the *Plain Dealer* guy, "Do you have anything much going today, John?"

He said, "No, just ten people killed on Granger Road in a truck accident."

I said, "Yeah, yeah, John."

John could make up fantastic stories. So I go into my room, and the phone rings. It's George Vukmanovich on the phone. He is hysterical!

"Where have you been? Everybody's been looking for you!"

Something tells me now that John wasn't kidding. And of course, he wasn't.

"Tanner's looking for you," George said.

"You haven't seen me. You haven't heard from me," I said. "Tell them you tried to reach me and I must've been on another story."

I didn't even know where Granger Road hill was and I didn't know where Marymount Hospital was, but I knew that people had been taken there. And I grabbed a map and the phone book and ran out to my little red VW and was on my way. And I did eventually find Granger Road hill. And of course, it was cordoned off by the cops and all the victims are gone and what have you. But there were a few people that helped out. So I started asking them what had happened, and found it pretty bad. And I asked someone, "Did you see the truck driver? Did you talk to the truck driver?"

They told me he was getting out of the cab and they ran up to him wondering if he was hurt, and he was just completely in shock, it seemed. He took a look around and he said, "Well, I guess I won't be driving no more."

Then I had to find my way to Marymount and I remember parking right in front of the emergency room door, and a cop came up, a security guard, made me move, and said, "You can't park here."

And the parking lot was loaded. I had to run a mile to get back to the emergency room. So I get in there, and nobody is around, I mean, nobody. There is one couple in evening dress, a guy and a woman, but otherwise, there was nobody. The nurses weren't even around. I thought at this time, "I'm going to get fired."

But I went up to the couple and asked, I said, "You know, I understand a bunch of people came in from Granger Road. There was a terrible accident there." They said, "Yeah. In fact, we're waiting to see what happened to our friends. We were following them to a wedding and they got hit."

Eventually people started coming out from the emergency room. I managed to get some really good stuff, I thought. So I started to relax and I called Al Thompson, who had been looking for me. And I called him and of course acted like I had been there all night. But I really didn't have anything from the cops yet. So I said, "The cops are kind of cleaning this up, and I can catch them a little later."

I got there early evening, but you have to understand, I was, like, three hours late realizing that everything had happened. I was lucky because an intern at the *Plain Dealer* was having a party that night, and the *PD* people were anxious to get out and go to that party, so by the time all these people are coming out of the emergency room and giving me good stuff, nobody from the *PD* or from TV—they're all gone, because it's too late for TV deadlines, and it's really almost past the *Plain Dealer* deadline.

All I know is that I worked until probably 4 in the morning, because I had to play catch-up with the police and everything and then write the story and all of that good stuff. So anyhow, the upshot of it was that I got a separate story on the human interest stuff, and the regular story, Page 1. And I think it was then, the following Monday, when I came in again, Al Thompson called. I thought, "Uh-oh, they found out what happened, and that I was nowhere around."

I get on the phone and he said, "Barb, you did a great job, great job. We put you in for eight hours overtime." Talk about pulling one out of the fire! I mean, you have no idea. I lost 10 years of my life then. Thereafter, I carried lots of dimes with me, back in the days when a phone call was a dime. And whenever I was out for a long time, I dropped many dimes calling around, trying to find out basic stuff if I wasn't in the office. It taught me a lesson.

MIKE ROBERTS
*Reporter, Editor,* Plain Dealer

The chief reporter for the *Press* then was Hilbert Black, a great guy and among the first black reporters on the newspapers. A federal court judge died around 5 o'clock in the afternoon and Hil knew that we were going to have to call the widow, too. He was going to make the initial call. He called me over and he said, "Now look, no matter how long you've been in the business, this is a hard thing to do, and I don't want this woman bothered with another phone call. So when I get off the phone, I'm going to give her to you so we won't have to bother her." That was really a class thing for him to do. I always remember him for that. You had terrific people like that who would help you along the way.

RUSS MUSARRA
*General Assignment Reporter,* Press

I was 21 and I got a chance to go to the police beat. We didn't call it crime reporting, we called it police reporting. And I worked with Hilbert Black. He was the chief police reporter for many, many years down there. Ernie Jackson—he was a Jehovah's Witness, I think. He left the business at some point. But he was older. I was 21 years old when I started. Ernie was already in his 30s. He'd been around the business. Of course, at that time, opportunities for blacks in the business weren't that great. Hilbert was black also—Hilbert and Ernie on staff was quite an achievement. I learned the nuts and bolts of reporting from guys like this.

WALLY GUENTHER
*Investigative, General Assignment Reporter,* Press

Hil Black was my chief on the police beat. Hilbert was a terrific reporter. The law enforcement people trusted him. They would call him. He never would break that confidence with them. I remember when I was on general assignment later, and most of the cops I would meet would always ask me if I knew Hil. Invariably, their response was, "What a gentleman." He had copy paper which he would fold up and he kept his notes on all that. He was very precise. Then later he went to the desk as assistant city editor and he was influential there, too. He was good with young reporters.

TOM SKOCH
*General Assignment Reporter,* Press

Hilbert was one of my biggest heroes, and still is. He was the best reporter. He was just so quiet and totally efficient. He'd walk out of the—we were based in the police station—and he'd walk out of the *Press* office and disappear for a half hour or an hour, and he'd be roaming the building talking to his contacts. And he'd come back and he'd have a notebook filled with very neat, almost like typewriter-type printing of the notes he'd taken. And he'd get on the phone and he'd call in all of these fabulous stories. I'm sitting there going, "I've been here all this time that he's been doing this and I've got nothing. How does he do that?" He was just fabulous.

STEVE ESRATI
*Copy Editor, Columnist,* Plain Dealer

On a hot summer night in 1965, a bunch of children stood on a corner of Superior Avenue. A convertible drove past and a man in the car shot a pistol at the children. The bullet he fired went into the scrotum of a young boy.

The boy was black; the man was white.

I was working the late shift on the copy desk and was told to write a four-column, 36-point headline for Page 1 about the incident. It would have been for the Sunday paper, but the story was ordered off the front page by a senior editor, Dave Rimmel, and eventually ended up at the back of the paper, near the obituaries.

Judged only on the basis of news value, that story belonged on the front page. Had it occurred in Bombay, nobody would have thought twice about running it there. But it happened in Cleveland and there wasn't any point in upsetting people, was there? You may want to know why stories often seem to be "buried" near the obituaries. Editors have no way of knowing who will die and so leave space for late obituaries. Late-breaking stories often go into that space. It is not an editorial judgment.

The incident led to the Hough riot a few weeks later. The shooting was something that upset people. The follow-up was also upsetting. A man showed up at a police station and handed the cops a gun, saying he was doing so because he understood that he was a suspect in the shooting of the boy and wanted the gun tested. The cops duly tested the gun, not knowing if it was the man's only gun, and reported that this absolved the man from suspicion because the volunteered gun did not match the gun that had shot the boy. No charges were ever laid in the case though there had been witnesses, a description of the car, a description of the man. It should not have come as a surprise to Cleveland that when the Hough riot took place, this man's considerable properties were fire-bombed.

STUART ABBEY

*Reporter, Copy Editor, Editor,* Plain Dealer

We didn't cover many East Side shootings or robberies. An occasional obit, maybe, if the person was extremely well known. If there was a shooting, the response was "Ah, that's another black." Blacks didn't exist. Until one of the big numbers guys got ambushed.

DAVID SARTIN

*Reporter,* Plain Dealer

There was a time, frankly, when you would call up with a homicide and city desk would ask you, is it a colored guy? Not all the black murders got in the paper, and there is much more sensitivity to that now, and that makes a better paper. So I'm one of the people that say that the paper is better than today, journalism is better, content is better.

DICK PEERY

*Reporter,* Plain Dealer

Staff diversity was always important. One example was in the 1970s when the two papers and three television stations rushed reporters to Collinwood High School for a decades-long rite-of-spring event: black and white students were fighting. Police made the white kids stay east of East 152nd Street and kept the black kids on the west side of the dividing line. Then the patrolmen took off their identifying badges and waded into the resisting black crowds to break them up. Only the two black journalists at the scene mentioned the lack of badges.

The next day I returned to the same situation, but this time the police were from a trained unit. They kept their badges on as they calmly walked up to the kids and gently asked them to please go home. The kids all said OK and walked away from the area. I wrote a story contrasting the effectiveness of the police methods, but it never ran. I never found out why.

DON BEAN

*Reporter,* Plain Dealer

It isn't good to get too close to your news sources because you depart from objectivity as a reporter. Now I like to think that Kent State University taught us objectivity above all, but being human, it's very, very difficult to be objective. I don't know anybody that's

100 percent objective, but I tried. I really strived to be. The night that Martin Luther King Jr. was assassinated I was at the police beat. The news was announced on the police radio. We monitored the police radio. There were cheers from somebody in the police car, and I did not report that and I didn't feel that it was necessary to report that because it would just create more problems. He was not one of the favorites of the policemen. I didn't encourage anybody to turn in that story.

DON BEAN
*Reporter,* Plain Dealer

Good old Bronco Brynes was a Cuyahoga Heights policeman—he just loved the media. I can't think of his given name. He'd call the media with stories. In fact, he'd call me at home and wake up my wife and say, "Tell Bean I got a hot one! I got a hot one!" And he did most times. One time he wanted me to do a story up there in the valley of the living dead, it was a landfill right there in Cuyahoga Heights, in the Cuyahoga Valley, where the winos lived. I just didn't like the idea. And Tony Natale did for the *Press* and, boy, he had a fabulous story out of it. Yeah, I got beat, sure.

JIM MARINO
*Criminal Courts Reporter,* Press

The most memorable story I ever covered was probably the Danny Greene/Cleveland Mafia continuing saga, how these two gangs—the Irish gang and the Italian gang—were battling it out on the East Side for control of the numbers business, and how that led to a number of deaths, including Shondor Birns, who was Cleveland's number one racketeer for decades. It led to Danny Greene's death; it led to Jack Licavoli's conviction for Greene's death. He was known on the street as Jack White, but his real name was Licavoli, and he was allegedly the "don" or the "capo" of Cleveland's Mafia family, which was known in FBI circles as the "gang that couldn't shoot straight."

Jack was in his 60s when he was convicted, and lived into his 70s in prison before he died. And his top lieutenant was Angelo Lonardo, and the Lonardo family goes back decades in Cleveland. It's difficult sometimes to sort out who's a cousin, who's a nephew, who's an uncle. But the old *Cleveland Press* morgue, where all the clips are just yellowed with age and if you'd touch them, they'd break into a million pieces, had clippings of the Lonardo family going back to, like, 1919, including one incident where a guy named Black Sam Todaro allegedly killed Little Angelo Lonardo's father, and he was going to get even with him by taking out Sam Todaro. He knew the barbershop where Sam had his office in the back, and with his mother's permission—imagine the mother giving her son permission to kill somebody—as the story is told, he just walked into the barbershop and killed Sam and then went out and drove home with his mother. Well, this is the same Angelo Lonardo that gets roped in with Licavoli in the Danny Greene trial.

This is an interesting story—I was trying to get on the defendants' good side at court, because I was sitting in the first seat back from the trial rail, and there's this whole table full of Mafia defendants and all their lawyers and everything, and every time they'd look at the media, they'd growl at you because they really didn't like the coverage.

So I was trying to get these guys to warm up to me because if I ever need to interview one of them, maybe they'd give me some words instead of spit at me. So I went over to the old morgue and I pulled out some old pictures of these guys when they were 20 years old. I actually stole them from the morgue and I gave them to them at the trial. And during the recess I said, "Hey, this is you when you were, like, 25 years old," and they looked at the pictures and they laughed out loud. From then on, Jack Licavoli used to bring candy for me because I gave him an old picture of himself.

The Danny Greene case just had so many peculiar angles to it. I took over the organized crime beat from a guy named Tony Tucci, and Tony was the one that tells me that whenever you get a phone call from a Mr. Patrick, that was Danny Greene's code name; that means he wants to talk to you about something. Danny Greene would send his two gunmen over, pick me up in a green stretch limo and we'd go to a restaurant, sometimes Pat Joyce's, and then Danny would walk out from nowhere and sit down and say, "Do you know who killed who? Well, let me tell you what's going on, but you can't quote me." And then, "Say hi to Tony for me." So I was being driven around town by Danny's gunmen for various meets with Danny throughout the year. And that was the start of my organized crime writing experience.

But everybody in Cleveland was getting blown up with car bombs back then, and the reason they called the Cleveland Mafia the "gang that couldn't shoot straight"—I can't remember who their target was, but a couple of Licavoli's boys were at the Cleveland airport one time and they had a bomb rigged to a guy's car in the airport parking lot, and they had their remote-control device in the hotel that looked down on the parking lot, and when the guy got in the car, they pressed the button and it didn't work. They go, "Shit, maybe we're too far away; maybe it's the distance." So they go running down the stairs as the car's slowly backing out of its parking space, and they're pressing the button again and it doesn't work. Then the car starts to drive away and they're running after the car, pressing the button and never got it to explode. It's almost like something you'd see on a comedy on TV.

# 4.

# "You never knew who was going to walk through . . ."

*If the police beat was the primary outpost for police and fire news, the city room was command headquarters for coverage of the entire city and beyond. Here, editorial writers pontificated on the issues of the day, and sportswriters and women's department writers struggled to make their contributions to the paper. Visitors were the famous and the infamous, entertainers and crooks, lawyers and judges, street people and society folk, each seeking something from the newspaper. From the city desk, stories were dished out, photographers assigned, and wire copy from UPI and Associated Press ripped from the teletype, studied and assigned a value in the next edition.*

*The guys at the rewrite desk either held phones to their ears and typed furiously or, with nothing to do, enjoyed a cigarette and a stroll around the place. Copy editors silently and determinedly cleaned up the grammatical and style mistakes of writers; they also wrote headlines and cutlines for the pictures. Tobacco smoke hung in the air, manual typewriters banged and clattered and chirped. The preferred method of communication was yelling. Telephones rang nonstop. Yet every day, from this madhouse came a good newspaper. Often filled with minor mistakes, sometimes with major mistakes. But every day, the fruit of this labor got out on time, filled with what the editors considered important or pleasurable for readers to know. No industry or business ever had the choreographed chaos, and daily success, of a newspaper city room.*

HARRIET PETERS

*Television Reporter,* Press

At first it was intimidating, you know, when you walk into this huge room with all this noise. That was in the days of the manual typewriters where the bells would ring when you shifted the carriage, and the phones all over the place, and at the *Press* at the time it was very informal so if somebody had a phone call and they were standing across the room, you didn't politely go up to them, you just shouted their last name across the room.

TOM SKOCH

*General Assignment Reporter,* Press

The city room was smoky, and noisy, too. Telephones were clanging because they were those loud old phones, and typewriters were manual typewriters. You had to hammer the keys: clackity, clackity, clackity, zzzz, zzzzz, bing! You know the sounds. Then the teletype machines were clattering away. There were three or four of those. Every once in a while there'd be bells going off—ding, ding, ding—when there was a special story that they wanted people to notice on the teletype machines. There were people talking and coming in and out. There was a huge amount of noise. You had to talk loud to be heard. The biggest shock when technology started coming was how quiet everything got. The silence was disturbing.

HELEN MOISE

*Food Writer,* Press

The city room was filled up in those days, and you never knew who was going to walk through there with whatever they had in their hands. Once, Jean Caldwell came in there with a chimpanzee and took him over to the city desk. At that time Bill Tanner was the city editor. Bill called me on the phone and said, "Helen, call my number and I want to see what this chimpanzee does." So I called the number, and the chimpanzee picked the phone up and answered the telephone. Then he went to the typewriter and started typing.

HARRIET PETERS
*Television Reporter,* Press

Once a year, the clowns from the circus came up to the city room. There would be maybe 10 of them, and they would be running all over the place, trying to make everybody laugh. Some of us were irritated because we were trying to write a story and here they are running around your desk. Where else could you work where you have 10 clowns running around, trying to make you happy?

DICK FEAGLER
*Reporter, Columnist,* Press

We had a guy who was a patient at a psychiatric hospital. His name was Bob and he would come in at least once a week. He always left a little bit forlorn. He would perch on the rim of the copy desk and just sit there. We thought he blended very well with the copy editors. But he would just sit there like one of the birds on a telephone wire, and sit there for several hours. Not that he bothered anybody. Then he'd just wander away again. One time I was leaving and it was raining, and he was coming in as I was going out. I said, "Gee, Bob, what brings you way down here on a day like this?" He said, "You have to get out of that place where I live. You can go crazy there." But one day he brought his girlfriend with him, and people thought he'd pushed the envelope too far. So we didn't see much of him after that.

Another guy who would come in with some regularity named Cyrus, Son of God. He was a madman. You'd see him on the street occasionally with a white robe and a white beard—a black guy with a white beard and a white robe with his leaflets. And he would just come up and run around passing out leaflets, "I am Cyrus, Son of God." He'd go around the track and back down the elevator or down the stairs and leave, and nobody would give a damn.

We had strippers coming in constantly. We had Irma the Body come in one day and she was walking a pink poodle, and they didn't know what to do with her so they gave her to Max Riddle, the dog writer.

Some guy came in one day with a gadget he had invented to teach dogs to retrieve. I don't know if it was spring-driven or what, but it threw this rubber wiener kind of thing out some distance and then the dog would run and get it. When it went off, the wiener shot across the city room and right through the glass in the artists' studio.

HARRIET PETERS
*Television Reporter,* Press

The way the city room was laid out, someone coming to be interviewed or photographed would walk all the way across the city room to the photographers' studio, which was in the back. So everybody got a good look, whether they were in the women's department or sports department or artists' room. Even the reporters in the UPI office got to stand up and look. One that stands out in my mind is Ann-Margret walking through the room trailing a chinchilla coat on her shoulder. When Roy Rogers came up to be interviewed, everybody wanted his autograph.

DON BEAN
*Reporter,* Plain Dealer

I joined the *Press* in 1954. I was a copy boy—$42.50 a week—with a degree from Kent State University, in journalism. The *Press* then was at the old building at East Ninth and Rockwell, wooden floors. Louie B. Seltzer was the god. I helped fill paste pots, run copy, wore a white shirt and a tie, tearing papers from hot off the press to the reporters so they could check their stories, and they'd fight like hell to get a paper from you and you'd look at your white shirt, and it was all dark from print. The presses were down in the basement, roaring and roaring away.

RUSS MUSARRA
*General Assignment Reporter,* Press

For me, being a copy boy was very exciting. When they wanted you to do something, they'd yell at the top of their lungs, "Boy!" And you better move to get there. The only one who didn't yell a lot was Louie Clifford, the city editor. He was probably the best writer that the *Cleveland Press* had, although he never wrote on a regular basis. I saw examples of his writing over time, and I was convinced that he was probably the best thing they had going. But he ran the city room, and occasionally he would crook his finger at you and you'd go over. The first time it happened, he just very casually said to me as I was walking by, "Russ, when you have a minute, I'd like you to do something." And I said, "Yes, sir." And I continued doing what I was doing for the next two or three or four minutes. And he looked over at me again and said, "Russ, now." I didn't have to be told a third time.

BOB YONKERS
*Reporter, Editor, Assistant to Editor,* Press

When I was hired, the *Press* was at East Ninth Street and Rockwell Avenue. It was on the fourth floor, no air conditioning, cuspidors all around the place and no air. It was boiling hot, you had to open the windows to get a breath of air. We had the windows open all the time. Any papers I didn't have weighted down with lead flew all over the place, and were full of dust.

HARRIET PETERS

*Television Reporter,* Press

Well, we had to do silly things like fill paste pots, because that's what the reporters used to paste their copy together from page to page. We sorted mail, got coffee for the reporters, and I was lucky that one of my jobs was leading tours. That was a real education, as I learned what happens to a piece of copy until the end when the paper comes off the presses. There is nothing like standing in the pressroom with those three-story presses and hearing the roar as they start running. I just loved that.

TOM SKOCH

*General Assignment Reporter,* Press

I think it was in 1972 that I got called in to work downtown. I was surrounded by my heroes. Louie Seltzer wasn't the editor. He had retired a few years before I started, but he'd come in from time to time and I was just in awe of the guy. I was afraid to talk to him. I was afraid to talk to a lot of these older guys, like Dick Maher, the political writer, and Milt Widder, a columnist. I worked with a lot of guys who are a little older than me that I kind of really looked up to—Norman Mlachak, you could hear angels sing when this guy wrote. From where I sat, Norman was across an aisle in front of me and behind me was Julian Krawcheck, the columnist, and next to him was Betty Klaric. And on the far side of Julian was Dick Feagler, who was a hot young maverick star reporter.

BILL WYNNE

*Photographer,* Plain Dealer

Roelif Loveland, or, "Lovie," as he was known, was a really tough man who wrote great poetry. He was a nationally respected writer and was one of one or two at the *PD* who worked on a contract basis. We would meet in the afternoon on occasion in the cafeteria over coffee. Lovie was a Marine in World War I and participated in the bayonet charges of Château-Thierry and Belleau Wood. In his younger drinking days he'd line up guys in the city room on Friday nights, and they'd push tables and chairs around to clear a space at the old building on East Sixth Street and Superior, roll up paper into a football, and—you may not believe this—play touch tackle. No one ever complained. He once stuffed a copy editor into a wastebasket upside down. He had played football at Oberlin College.

TONY TOMSIC

*Photographer,* Press

Norm Mlachak was a very good reporter. He was good with people stories—especially when there was a tragedy or something, But Norm knew I would not allow smoking in my car, and one time Norm and I went out on a run. There was a stickup on Public Square and we were there for the final edition. We drove over there, and when he got in my car—it was in the summertime—it was after lunch, and I had gone down to my uncle's meat market on St. Clair and bought a couple pounds of Slovenian sausage and had them in the trunk. Well, they were getting a little warm and the smell of the garlic and everything—there was quite a smell in the car. And he made a point of mentioning how it smelled like that. He said, "I don't know if I can put up with that."

As it turned out, I guess the robbers were confronted and left. There was basically no story. So when I got back to the darkroom about 20 minutes later, the phone rings and it's Louie Clifford. Clifford says, "There's a bulletin here on the bulletin board that Norm Mlachak wrote that you may want to read." Of course, I had no idea what it was. When I went out there, Norman had wrote a bulletin just like he would for Page 1 but complaining about the smell of the sausage, and that he was no longer going to put up with it and that we have to do something about it. I think I still have that thing at home somewhere. Working there was fun. It really was. You know, there were times when you'd really give it your all.

GEORGE VUKMANOVICH
*Copy Boy,* Press

Isi Newborne would come in and it would be late at night, like about 11 at night or something like that, and start doing his work, and he'd say, "Well, it's time for my exercise," so he's puffing on this big cigar and running around the *Press* city room. He said he had to get his exercise, do his jogging, while puffing on this huge stogie. I think he was in his 60s, but he looked good.

JIM STRANG
*Reporter,* Plain Dealer

I remember reading, in the old police beat clip books, a series the *Press* did—it had to be in the mid-'50s—about some brothel on Prospect Avenue that had an underage girl in it. And it was a blow-by-blow account of what was going on in the house. And I said, "Damn, this is journalism. This is crusading newspapering. Show people what's going on on this planet." We wouldn't touch that story today with a pole of any length.

TOM SKOCH
*General Assignment Reporter,* Press

When I started, it was back in the day with manual typewriters and on paper, and I had scissors and a paste pot on my desk. It was really the Stone Age. The first thing that happened, the first technological advance, was that they replaced the manual typewriters with electric typewriters, the IBM Selectrics. That, for some of the older guys, was it. That was a hurdle they couldn't get over. Bus Bergen could not, would not, did not want to go anywhere near one of these Selectrics. So he'd write his stuff the old way, on a manual, and then hand it to one of us kids and we'd type it in with the computer coding that you had to put on the stories after a certain time, because they'd run the stories through an optical scanner and then put it into the computer system that the copy desk began using.

MIKE ROBERTS
*Reporter, Editor,* Plain Dealer

I was sent over to the courthouse one day. I didn't know anything about the criminal court. The day city editor said, "Check in at the pressroom." Well, it's 1 o'clock in the afternoon and I opened the pressroom door, and it's dark and I clicked the lights on and there's a bed in there and there's a guy lying in the bed sleeping. The guy wakes up and says, "Turn those goddamn lights off, and who the hell are you?" I say, "I'm Mike Roberts from the *Plain Dealer.*" He says, "You know, all you assholes these days with your rep ties and tweed coats are looking like fraternity pledges."

It was Bus Bergen, who I knew of but never met. Bergen was a legendary reporter. I remember as a kid, watching [the television show] "The Big Story," brought to you by Pall Mall. Bergen was on two of those. That was on national television. He was like Superman. So I said, "Mr. Bergen, I'm sorry. I apologize."

"That's all right," he said, "There's a bottle in the desk. Take a drink if you want, and hey kid, don't break your neck running around trying to get a story. They call me first."

# 5.

# "It seemed like an easy job."

## [ GETTING STARTED IN NEWSPAPERS ]

*Lots of them fell in love with newspapers when, as kids, they delivered the paper. Many declared journalism a college major; plenty arrived and succeeded with little more than a high school diploma. Harriet Peters, after college, applied at a public relations firm, where she was told to join a newspaper for experience. She did and she never left. Doris O'Donnell was a city room Rosie the Riveter. She didn't leave, either. All came with an insatiable curiosity. Many, but not all, knew how to touch type. For almost all, the job seemed a natural and normal fit.*

STUART ABBEY
*Reporter, Copy Editor, Editor,* Plain Dealer

After hanging around a while as a copy boy and watching reporters, it occurred to me, "Hey, there's nothing to this." I had taken a news-writing class and a feature-writing class and by that time, I knew how to write a story.

DORIS O'DONNELL
*Reporter,* News

Sam Slotky hired me for the Heights *Sun Press.* Fifty cents a week. I was the first reporter to cover Cain Park; I covered the first shovelful of dirt. It was very exciting because I was now a newspaperwoman. I was also editor of my high school paper, the *Rhodes Review*. I loved Sam. He was a nice little pot-bellied guy. He taught me how to gamble. He always had Irish Sweepstakes tickets that we all bought. And he'd play the horses and he'd play the numbers.

JIM NAUGHTON
*Reporter,* Plain Dealer

J. Edgar Hoover got me started. When I was in the 3rd or 4th grade, about 8 years old, I wanted to emulate the people who were lionized on the radio in the show "The FBI in Peace and War." So I wrote to J. Edgar Hoover and asked him how I could become an FBI agent. Several weeks later in the mail there was an enormous packet of data and a letter supposedly from J. Edgar, telling all about how great the agency was and what they looked for in agents. The gist was that you needed a master's degree in accounting or a law degree.

Well, I lost interest in anything that would require that many more years of schooling. I guess I was moping in class and my teacher, Miss Ryan, at St. Mary's School in Painesville, asked me why. I told her about the FBI letter. She said something like, "Aw, you should be a writer." From that moment on I started focusing on being a reporter. I had one of those rubber-type child's printing presses and put out a little neighborhood paper. I put a make-believe press card in my Sunday church hat. I worked on the Harvey High School *Har-Binger* newspaper and became its editor.

And in one of the luckiest streaks, I walked into the *Painesville Telegraph* while I was a high school junior and asked for work. They hired me for 75 cents an hour to take high school sports info and write little stories for the sports section. And every summer from 1955 through 1960 I was the go-to person as vacation sub for the *Telegraph*—courthouse, city hall, cops, fashion photography, proofreading in the back shop, general assignment, sports, even editing the Geauga County *News-Leader,* one of the other small papers the Rowley family owned. It was a great experience and introduction to the craft.

BILL BARNARD
*Reporter, Editor,* Plain Dealer

I wrote for the St. Joe's school paper, and I really liked it. I didn't have the money to go to college, but I had a relative who was a shift supervisor at Fisher Body who got me a job on the assembly line. First I was a packer. We would get semi-trailers de-livering boxes of nuts and bolts. I could empty the trailer in one morning, but I was told to stretch it out for a full day, that if we went too fast, we would lose jobs. I wanted to earn money to go to college, not to work at an assembly plant. So I saved enough to go to college and decided to go into journalism. Everyone thought I was crazy when I quit to go to John Carroll and then got this low-paying job working as a copy boy at the *Plain Dealer.*

ROBERT FINN
*Critic,* Plain Dealer

My mother was involved in journalism in kind of a peripheral way. I'm from Boston, and my mother was the secretary to a man named Harry Nelson, who was a financial columnist for an out-fit called the Boston News Bureau, which was sort of a Boston outpost of the old *Barron's Weekly* financial paper. That's how I learned to type, by going into the office where she worked, and climbing up on the typewriter. I type like all journalists do to this very day—very fast and very inaccurately—with about three and a half fingers on each hand. But my mother was in the journalism business, so I fell in love with journalism at that point. And, of course, I've always loved music, which also came mostly from my mother. She was a decent pianist and had been a subscriber to the Boston Symphony for a good many years. And I guess I just sort of inherited it with my mother's milk. So what do you do when you're interested in journalism and love to write and love music? You become a music critic. That's what happened to me.

FRANK ALEKSANDROWICZ
*Photographer,* Press

I lost my job on January 1, 1957. I worked on the Erie, Pa. paper from '41 to that period, taking away the two terms of service in the military. And I lost my job and I didn't sleep that night. I slept in Normandy, but I didn't sleep that night, I was worried. I put out feelers to different editors of the night chain starting in Akron, down to Charlotte, N.C., down to Miami—*Free Press*—all the good papers. They were a damn good chain, and I knew their papers. But anyway, by accident, my wife's mother, who was from Belgium, lived with us, and she had a job as a nanny in Shaker Heights. I had a call from my wife, who said that her mother heard from her employer that the *Press* was looking for a photographer. I went to the *Plain Dealer* and they had no opening. So, I came up three times to the *Press*. It was Louie Seltzer, down to the photographer, and I think the janitor came in to see my work. I had full pages of pictures that all these people saw. I covered every facet of newspaper photography from sports on through. And so I was hired to start in February. I think it was on Lincoln's birthday, in 1957.

DICK PEERY
*Reporter,* Plain Dealer

After about three years, a new *Call and Post* city editor who didn't like me—probably with good reason—prompted me to apply to the *Plain Dealer*, where they paid twice as much. I thought my clippings from the *Call and Post* were good enough to get the job, but I will never know for sure. The day before my scheduled interview, Mayor Carl Stokes issued an analysis of hiring practices at the *Plain Dealer* and concluded that there was rampant racial discrimination. I hadn't known about the study and was afraid it would look like a setup, but realized I had nothing to lose. The interviewers did not bring it up. They just wanted the names of *Plain Dealer* reporters who knew me. Bob McGruder, Ned Whelan and Tom Andrejewski all vouched for my credibility and I got the job.

HELEN MOISE
*Food Writer,* Press

I went to Kent State University and graduated in '57, with a degree in home economics and business. A friend of mine who worked at the *Plain Dealer* in the food department called me in Akron and said there's an opening for you—well, not you—but there's an opening for a home ec writer, food writer at the *Cleveland Press.* And I said, "Well, I don't know anything about writing about food or about journalism." The *Press* was on Ninth Street then. That was the new building. And so I came in and went straight in to the associate editor. He was sitting there with his legs up on the table, his shirts sleeves rolled up like all newspapermen, and he said, "Okay. Tell me why you want to be a reporter."

"I know absolutely nothing about it," I said. "I didn't major in journalism, but I do know a lot about food. My father was a chef in the restaurant business and I majored in home economics and I think I could make food come to life because that's what I know."

They asked me to write a story about cooking fish. The first thing that came to my mind was that fish smells up the whole house so how do you cook it so that it doesn't smell up the house. So I made up all this stuff on the typewriter and handed this story in. Two weeks later they hired me. Anyway, I started there on February 9, 1962.

BOB YONKERS
*Reporter, Editor, Assistant to Editor,* Press

I graduated from John Marshall High School and started looking for a job in 1933 and I applied at the *Press*, the *News* and the *Plain Dealer*. The *Plain Dealer* said that they would like to see me get a college degree, go get some journalism, and so on. I had not worked in journalism at school at all. I had nothing to do with the school paper. When I applied, the *News* said they just weren't hiring. Then suddenly, the paper changed edition times—from 7:30 in the morning to 10:30 for the first edition. And for some reason, they needed more copy boys, and I was one of those picks. When I was interviewed by Louis Seltzer, he asked me if I was naturally timid and I said, "Only in your presence, sir."

MIKE ROBERTS
*Reporter, Editor,* Plain Dealer

I wanted to be a newspaper reporter since I was a kid, about 10 years old, delivering the *Press*. There was never any other thing I wanted to do. The city was delivered to you every day in that newspaper. It had these wonderful stories about Shondor Birns, and mysteries like Beverly Potts. The city looked very exciting to me from Garfield Heights. And reporting was something that I really wanted to do. I'd go downtown—you still had streetcars in those days—and walk around. I'd look at Short Vincent Street, where the *Press* did so many stories. Of course I'd be afraid to walk down that street. But it seemed so exciting to be a reporter. And I continued to pursue that.

I went to college at Baldwin-Wallace. I worked on the school paper from the day I got there until the day I graduated. But when I was in school, I worked a lot for the *Plain Dealer* on the weekends. I did sports writing. I wanted to be a sportswriter for a while. I'd work on Friday and Saturday nights. I'd take the football or baseball or basketball scores. I got to know the guys there. But there were no jobs when I got out of college. It was a tough time, particularly at the *Plain Dealer*, where people seemed to hold jobs forever. You had a lot of 60-, 70-year-old reporters. And then suddenly everybody seemed to be retiring and there were openings. I worked for a year on the Ashtabula *Star Beacon* before I came to the *Plain Dealer*. I was disappointed my old paper, the *Press*, wouldn't hire me.

TONY NATALE

*Investigative, General Assignment Reporter,* Press

I joined the *Press* around 1960. I'd been going to the University of Toledo and I quit because I was getting bored with college and I always enjoyed writing, but I never thought I'd be a writer. I thought I'd be an ad salesman. And I bumped into a family friend of ours who was a councilman on the West Side. He brought me in to the *Press* office and introduced me to Louie B. Seltzer, and encouraged Seltzer to hire me, which he did. I started as a copy boy in those days. I was a copy boy for about 10 months and I realized that I did not want to be an ad salesman, that I wanted to be a reporter.

BRENT LARKIN

*Politics,* Press

I was born in Cleveland. I went to college at Ohio U., and then I got a law degree up the street. I majored in journalism at OU. In hindsight, I know that you're supposed to major in English. I think the journalism schools do a great job. I don't have the low opinion of journalism degrees that some people have.

I shouldn't have been hired at the *Press*, but that has nothing to do with what I majored in.

I was a terrible student. I had every bad habit in the world except for drugs. I didn't go to class. I graduated with about a 2.2 or a 2.3 at an easy school. I had a job interview at an employment agency after I graduated. I was on the four-and-a-half-year plan. So I get off the Shoreway and I see I'm real early. I turn left on East Ninth Street and there's the *Press* building on the left-hand side. Well, I have a degree in journalism. I'm going to go in there and see if anything happens.

I didn't wait 15 minutes. The managing editor at the time was Dick Campbell, who was a graduate of Ohio University, and who later served on the board of trustees at Ohio University. Dick Campbell loved Ohio University and its people, and the newsroom was full of them at the time. He never asked me about my grades. He never asked me a thing that was relevant. He said, "Come back on January 2, and you start." I never went to the employment agency. I started on January 2 of 1970. Then later Bill Tanner told me, "By starting on the second, you got screwed out of some vacation. It's determined by how many years you've been with the company on January 1." Still, there is no reason in the world that Campbell should've hired me.

HARRIET PETERS

*Television Reporter,* Press

I majored in journalism at Bowling Green State University with the intention of going into public relations. I thought PR would be fun. I was thinking about fun, not money. After graduating in June, I started at the *Press* in July as a copy boy. The reason I ended up at the paper was that when I went to interview for public relations jobs at companies in Cleveland, they said that you need to have a writing background and we suggest that you get a job at a newspaper. Just before I got the job I was offered a job at a utility company, and I am just so glad I didn't take it. I would have had a lot more money, but that wasn't important.

Once I got to the *Press* I never wanted to leave. In fact, I always figured that they would have to carry me out, you know, that I would die there.

TONY TOMSIC
*Photographer,* Press

I got interested in photography in high school—actually in junior high school. I played a little football, but when I was practicing the extra point, I got blindsided and wore a back brace for about 15 months. And I had nothing to do during those 15 months, so I started taking pictures.

JIM STRANG
*Reporter,* Plain Dealer

I was going to be a high school history teacher because I loved American history, I loved world history. I was going to the Ashtabula branch campus of Kent. Without the branch campuses that Jim Rhodes put in, I never would've gone to college. It was that touch and go. In those days, 1963, tuition was $123 a quarter, and those were real dollars. I was almost in my third year at the branch and I was out of money and needed a job. The [Ashtabula] *Star Beacon* put up a job notice on the bulletin board. They were looking for a reporter at the radio station and a reporter for the *Star Beacon.*

So I called them. They had filled the radio job, so they asked me about working for the newspaper. I said, "Sure." And this was my first sales job ever. I knew two things about newspapers, both from watching "Superman" on TV—one was what you wrote, you called, "copy," and you put "30" at the end of it. And that was what I knew about newspapers. So I went in and he asked me, "Have you ever had any experience?" I said, "No. But I can write." They hired me for a $1.50 an hour, part-time, no benefits, just straight pay, four hours a day. I went in the first day and they sat me down at this desk. And God as my witness, I looked at that typewriter, and I panicked, because the place was so cheap that on the type-writer, all the letters on the keys had been worn off. I was looking at an array of perfectly black keys. I didn't know how to type and had no idea of what I was looking at. Fortunately, the desk ahead of me was close, and that typewriter had the letters on the keys. So I looked down at those keys. Do you know how long it takes to write a story when you're looking for every key? Fortunately, they didn't want much. And after a month or two, they shifted typewriters around, and I got one that had letters on it. My first big story out there was when they got 24 inches of snow on the 23rd of March, 1966. I went out and photographed it and came back and wrote it and I got it across the top of the page—my first byline. It was just amazing!

FRED MCGUNAGLE

*Suburban Editor, General Assignment,* Press

I had a *Press* route when I was a kid, and somehow then I started thinking that this is where I would like to work. I was fascinated by it, and when I got to John Carroll, I worked on the school paper; I was eventually editor of it. On one occasion I had taken the 32C downtown from John Carroll and boarded the Greyhound for the trip back to Rocky River, and we were leaving the station, and going through downtown and picking people up in the twilight, and I was listening to these two young fellows behind me who were all excited. I listened to them, and it turns out these were newspaper reporters, I'm not sure for what paper, and the one guy was really excited because he was pretty sure he had caught a public official that he covered in some sort of betrayal of the public trust, and he was in the process of nailing this down. And the other guy was just fascinated listening to him. And I looked around the bus and there were all these people sitting—mostly staring, either out the window or into space. They had all left their dull jobs and they're riding home to dinner and their families so they could come alive again. And here behind me, these two young guys are still bubbling over about their job. And that was something that helped confirm what I already thought I wanted to do.

**V. DAVID SARTIN**
*Reporter,* Plain Dealer

I have a fond memory when I was a little kid of going to this one lady's house, and I always looked forward to it because she had *Time, Look, Saturday Evening Post* and *Life* magazine, and I used to lay on the carpet and just read those magazines and many times kept looking at the pictures. I have the fondest memories of my childhood reading those magazines and looking at the pictures. I knew that I wanted to be a reporter from my earliest childhood when I had this fascination with the whole notion to go to talk to people, asking them questions, writing it down, listening to them, paying attention. And it came true.

**BOB YONKERS**
*Reporter, Editor, Assistant to Editor,* Press

Being a *Press* reporter, the neighbors all thought I was a big shot, and when I started getting a byline, that's when my family thought I was the greatest.

**BOB AUGUST**
*Sports Editor, Columnist,* Press

I had an uncle who was a newspaperman in Pittsburgh for the Pittsburgh *Press.* We'd go up there and visit him in Pittsburgh. He was doing well in his job. He was coming up in that business. He took us to the Pittsburgh *Press.* That was the first newspaper I was ever in. And he just seemed to me to live kind of an exciting life in relation to what I was seeing. He took us up to the *Press* and he took us to the composing room. He told the guy on the linotype machine that he wanted him to print this line. He said that Frank August, of Cleveland—that was my father—was in Pittsburgh this weekend visiting his equally distinguished brother. I thought it was kind of an interesting way to make a living. You didn't have to work too hard and it seemed like a lot of fun. I kind of had an idea that might be something I'd like to do.

BOB DOLGAN

*Sports Reporter, Columnist,* Plain Dealer

I went to John Carroll University and was one of the few guys from my working-class neighborhood on East 65th and St. Clair to go to college. I majored in English because it was my best subject, but I really didn't know what kind of work I was going to do. Once in a while one of my buddies would say, "What are you going to college for? You're going to work in a factory with the rest of us." That terrified me. I thought I would look ridiculous if I had a college degree and worked in a shop. So I used to think about what I was going to do with myself when I finished. I said, "I know what I'd like to be, a sportswriter." But I just assumed that you had to know somebody to get on a paper. It seemed like such an easy job.

But I gave it a try and got a job at the old Geneva [Ohio] *Free Press* for 40 bucks a week. I covered sports, the mayor's office and even took and developed photos. After about 15 months there I wrote to Gordon Cobbledick, sports editor of the *Plain Dealer*, and asked him for a job. To my surprise, he called me in and hired me.

BILL TANNER

*Reporter, City Editor,* Press

I'm a native Clevelander. I was born in 1925 on upper Kinsman. I went to school at John Adams High School. I went to college at Western Reserve. My degree was in English and science.

When I was a kid, I liked writing and I liked reading. I started reading the comics and then the sports pages. I remember when I was very young, the boys going through yelling when the Lindbergh baby was kidnapped—I remember that, they were yelling, "Extra! Extra!" That was exciting. And so when I went to junior high school—Alexander Hamilton—I joined the junior high school newspaper. When I went to high school, I knew then that I liked journalism, so I immediately tried out for the *John Adams Journal.* And Verda Evans—a wonderful person around town, became head of the English department for the Cleveland Public Schools—she worked with the *Press* during World War II when there was a shortage of reporters. She came on the *Press* and worked summers, even some during the school year. She was a wonderful teacher, and we were good friends since I'd been editor of her high school papers, and then we remained friends after that. She was a great influence on me.

Right out of high school, I went and applied for a job at the *Press* and Louie Seltzer hired me as an office boy.

GEORGE CONDON

*Columnist,* Plain Dealer

I worked at Mount Union College in Alliance, Ohio, as their PR man. I was there for four or five months, and the managing editor of the *Columbus Citizen*, Doc Weimer, called me and said you got a job, George. Better get here. The newspapers were losing men to the service, and I had been rejected because of perforated eardrums, so I was a safe bet.

I went to Columbus and walked in on Doc Weimer for my new job, and he covered his face with his hands, and said, "George, I'm sorry. See that son of a bitch over there? He's the guy you were suppose to succeed, replace, but he failed his physical so there is no opening." I went to work for the Federal Agriculture

Department—and I should have stayed with that job. The *Plain Dealer* then called and the *Springfield Sun*; each offered me a job. It was wartime, and I went to Cleveland and was interviewed by Jim Collins, who was a very impressive guy, I thought. Very intelligent individual. He offered me $50 a week—now remember, I was making $65! But I took the $50 and I was a reporter for only three years, and Paul Bellamy made me the radio/television editor. That was a new job, television.

V. DAVID SARTIN
*Reporter,* Plain Dealer

You had to learn your way around very quickly. You learned a lot of tricks. You learned which of the old-timers were going to be mentors and who was going to teach you things. You learned great stories about how to get by in the big city. You learned some very serious practical lessons, like never leave home without a pocket full of dimes, because it was long before cell phones and you had to move fast and get to a pay phone and call people, and you burned through a pocketful of dimes every day. You learned well where all the public bathrooms were because if you had to take a leak, you had to take a leak, so you learned which gas stations were open late at night and which public libraries had a back door that they let you slip in and go to the john, maybe there would be a convenient pay phone right there. You learned that kind of thing. You learned how to get from downtown to the airport fast by going along Berea Road, and skip 71, because you can get out there just as fast. You learned about side streets and you learned quickly. It was great to have some of the old-timers guiding you.

BARBARA WEISS
*Reporter,* Press

I didn't have a degree. Previous to the *Press*, I worked at the Cleveland Bar Association as a secretary/receptionist. But

I wanted to write, so I applied at both the *PD* and the *Press*. It didn't look like I was going to get into either one as a writer because I had no college.

I finally got hired doing clerical work for the *Press* business department. I thought, "At least I have my foot in the door." A year and a half later, I started sending notes to Louie Seltzer, to Norm Shaw—and by then I was going to night school for a Bachelor of Arts. I took English and journalism. Anyway, in these notes, I was begging them for a job. I wanted to write, could they find me a place upstairs. Finally, Norm Shaw talked to me and said that Louie had talked to him. And I even had short stories and stuff to show I could write. I mean, I really had a lot of chutzpah back then when I was a kid. The union wasn't happy with it because my pay was going to be reduced. They were going to give me a job as a copy girl and if I worked out, fine, and if not, I was gone. Well, it did work out. And I was there, I bet less than six weeks, and there was an opening in the home magazine.

And I was working as a copy girl and filling in on the home magazine. Then Norm Shaw came up to me one morning and said, "They're happy with you. You got the job permanently. And you are now a reporter."

I was absolutely exhilarated when he said that to me. I went out to lunch and celebrated. I came back. It was around 1 P.M. Remember the old bells that used to go off when there was an important story coming across the teletype machine? Well, if there was a really important story, bells would go off so that all the editors would be alerted to look and see what's coming across.

And the next thing I hear is that Kennedy's been shot. So I always remember that day when I was made a reporter. All hell broke out; everybody's scrambling. Everybody worked so hard. Seltzer scrapped the last edition, I believe. He remade the whole thing to have the assassination. That was quite a start for me. I was happy one moment, and pretty darn sad the next.

# 6.

# "There's always another deadline . . ."

*In addition to keeping track of crime and politics (often one and the same), the city room had desks for all sorts of specialists. Aviation, business, stamps, fashion, government, society, religion, common pleas and federal court, nationalities, obituaries, the military, suburbs, education, columnists, medicine, labor, and the fine arts—and general assignment. At one time both the* Press *and* Plain Dealer *had dog writers.*

LOU MIO
*Reporter,* Plain Dealer

At that time, the biggest story that I probably worked on in Lake County was the Hoffman murder case—Howard Thomas Hoffman, a young man. I think it was an insurance scam which he and his wife were involved in, only his wife didn't get charged with anything. We had a story about a house fire in Mentor. We went over there and there were two people dead in the fire, this man and this woman—Howard Thomas Hoffman II and his wife. We thought it was a fire—two people dead in a fire. The *Plain Dealer* kid who was delivering the papers saw the fire. They took the bodies out of there. After the autopsy, they found, I think, three bullets in the father and two bullets in the mother. And it was the kid, subsequently, we found out, who murdered his mother and father, using soft lead bullets, figuring that they would melt in the fire and the evidence would be gone, and he'd get the insurance. Well, he killed his mother and father. And they had him. They got him.

That was in '72, I believe. That was Page 1 for a long time. I was in the basement of the Lake County Courthouse, and an assistant prosecutor friend of mine came by and told me, "They found three slugs in him and two in her. But you didn't hear it from me."

Bingo! We were off and running. The *Telegraph* had two really good pictures of the parents—the father was a bigwig at Lubrizol, which is out in Wickliffe. We had shitty photos of the parents. So I called the editor of the *Telegraph*, who was a friend of mine. This was in the afternoon. We were going to get it first the next morning. I said, "I'll trade you a piece of information if you'll let me borrow those two photos of Mr. and Mrs. Hoffman."

He agreed and we went out to lunch. He gave me the photos. I said that they found three slugs in him and two in her. I don't know if we got to lunch or not. But his eyes popped. I said, "Yeah. I just got the tip . . . These people were murdered, obviously."

I knew that we'd have the story first because it was in the middle of the afternoon and the *Painesville Telegraph* would have to follow us. I said, "Okay. I'm going to give you a head start here, so that you don't have to start tomorrow morning. You can start this afternoon." But I got two good pictures.

TOM SKOCH

*General Assignment Reporter,* Press

In the Lake County Bureau, we had three reporters and then a circulation lady and a secretary who doubled as a receptionist and teletype operator. This was like in the Stone Age. We'd type our stories on manual typewriters and hand them to the

secretary. She'd turn around and type them on the teletype machine and they'd show up on the other end in the office of the
*Press* downtown. There'd be messages going back and forth on
the teletype. It was kind of like e-mail messages back and forth,
only before e-mail.

BRENT LARKIN
*Politics,* Press

I went to suburbs for less than a year, where I worked for Fred
McGunagle, who taught you a lot about reporting. He taught you
how to cover a beat. He was a stickler and a big pain in the ass,
but he was also a good teacher.

I worked very hard in the suburbs. I'm not one to blow my
own horn, but I broke a lot of stories in the suburbs—in Garfield
Heights, in Solon, in Bedford Heights. Nobody went to jail, but I
worked really hard. By that time I had become a real hard worker.
I didn't work hard in college, but I worked real hard at reporting.
If you worked real hard and had a little ingenuity, you were going
to get good stories. I developed a lot of sources. I liked to work
the phones. Some of the sources that I developed in the suburbs,
I still have today.

JIM STRANG
*Reporter,* Plain Dealer

A lot of reporters called Fred McGunagle "McGoo." If you
wanted to learn the craft, you listened to what McGoo had to
say. He made your copy better. There aren't many editors that really made your stuff better when they touched it. But McGoo was
just—of course, in those days, burbs were for beginners. After
you went to police beat, you went to the burbs. They sorted out
who could do stuff and who couldn't. I think his line was "There
are seventeen basic suburban stories. Just the numbers change."
And he knew the calendar that the government runs on—when

the tax assessments were done and when various things happen and who you should talk to. But that guy was one of the best
teaching editors I ever worked for. And did you ever see that guy
play softball? The *Press* had a softball team. It was the damned-
est thing—I was the third-string right fielder because I loved the
game, but I had no athletic ability. But McGoo, with those coke-
bottle-bottom glasses, was the best place hitter I think I've ever
seen in softball. He'd stand there at the plate, put the bat down
between his legs, put his hands in his pants and hitch them up
over his potbelly, stare out at the pitcher, and then drop the ball
over the second baseman's head. It was just what you would not
expect from him.

LOU MIO
*Reporter,* Plain Dealer

Going to the suburbs was a somewhat lateral move. I think
it was general assignment more than anything else, working
mostly for women, as a matter of fact. It was always changing.
"We'll cover it this way, and we'll cover this; we'll cover it this
way, we'll cover it that way." They're still screwing around trying
to figure out how to cover the suburbs.

MIKE ROBERTS
*Reporter, Editor,* Plain Dealer

When I came home from covering the Vietnam War they sent
me to the Washington bureau for two years and I covered the
White House one of those years. It was a good experience but it
was a shitty job. I don't know why anybody wants to spend their
lives covering the place. You're a captive. You're totally captive.
If you're with the *New York Times*, maybe you had some clout.
The *Plain Dealer* had no clout in Washington. One White House
secretary thought it was the *Plane Dealer* and that I worked for
an airline.

But sometimes you'd get a lead on a good story. One day a source in the Pentagon who I knew from Vietnam called. "The White House is staffed with a number of young lieutenants trained in intelligence. They're all politically connected. You've got two guys from Baltimore and a guy from Cleveland who are spending their war in comfort. You didn't hear it from me."

Turns out one of the kids there in a safe job was the son of the number-two guy at Jones Day, who had been the undersecretary of Treasury at one time. So I called Nixon's press secretary, Ron Ziegler. And I loved to annoy Ziegler. I said, "Hey, can I come over? I want to tell you something." He said, "What do you want to talk about?" I said, "We want to know why you have these guys in the White House when they should be in Vietnam?" There was a lot of dancing around. That was probably the best story in the year that I was there.

BOB YONKERS

*Reporter, Editor, Assistant to Editor,* Press

David Dietz—"Doctor" Dietz—was a very nice person, very intelligent [Pulitzer Prize for reporting, 1937]. He rose to stardom when we started getting into the space age. He was science editor, and when I was in public service, we would sponsor—everybody would bring their telescopes to either Edgewater Park or Gordon Park on certain nights when David Dietz would tell us that there was going to be a spectacular something in the sky. And people would turn out in droves just because Dave Dietz told them to. There were telescopes all over the place.

JIM RYAN

*Action Line Editor,* Press

Action Line was funny. Tom Boardman was editor. He had gone to Dallas and they had a thing like Action Line, and he just went ape over that and thought, well, here was the answer to everything. Well, he went around and asked who could write. I was in public service, and I wanted to be director of public service. Boardman called me in and said, "I've asked all over the paper, and you'll be delighted to know that everyone thinks you can handle a new feature, 'Action Line.'"

And I said, right off the top of my head, "No, thank you."

"What's the matter?" he asked.

And I said, "Well, I think it's going to be popular for a while and will fast fade and end up in the funny pages."

He kind of smiled, and he said, "Well, I still want you to do it, and there's a $10 a week raise if you do it." And of course, that was like heaven.

I set up the whole operation. I got the tape-recording machine in the office back there. People would call me with questions. They'd call or write. And it was phenomenal at first. It was unbelievable. The mail came in by the canvas sack. And of course 98 percent of this stuff was absolutely unusable—you know, "What color are Mary Pickford's eyes?" He gave me an assistant—somebody opened the mail and everything. And I wrote this stuff like crazy.

DARRELL HOLLAND
*Religion Editor,* Plain Dealer

I got a call from some guy who said he died and came back and would like to talk with me about his experience. I thought, how the hell do I do that story? Who do you check with to see if it's true? So I told him I wasn't interested. Next day, front page of the *Press.*

BOB DANIELS
*Reporter, Rewrite,* Plain Dealer

In those days, not only did the *Plain Dealer* have a religion writer, they also had a Catholic editor. Yeah, that was the job title.

Edythe Westenhaver was the Catholic editor when I first started there back in '64. And she later got a job at the Vatican.

DARRELL HOLLAND
*Religion Editor,* Plain Dealer

A preacher lady kept bothering me with long phone conversations. One day she called so many times I essentially hung up on her. A little while later, Bob McGruder, the managing editor, came over to my desk and said, "Did you hang up on someone?" I told him yes, and why. He told me, we don't do that and we can't do that. He went back to his office.

A day or so later, he came over and said, "Now I understand. I got another call from that woman, and she told me my mom has cancer and that she's praying for her. You're off the hook."

JIM STRANG
*Reporter,* Plain Dealer

I was never involved with the really big investigative stuff or any of that. I admired those guys, but I was the daily hit guy. I loved General Assignment. You didn't have to kiss anybody's ass. You didn't have to cultivate all the sources. You just went in. They'd say, "Hey, call this guy and see if there's a story." And if there was a story there, you wrote it and you went home at night, and the next day was a new adventure.

FRED MCGUNAGLE
*Suburban Editor, General Assignment,* Press

I was the early man on the city desk. I would get into work at 5:30 in the morning and find memos from the night police reporters. The early reporter, which was usually Wally Guenther, would be in at 6:30, and my job was to go through the memos and find something to send him out on. The early reporter's job was like making a silk purse out of a sow's ear.

TEDDI GIBSON-BIANCHI
*Entertainment Critic, Medical Reporter,* Press

I was a medical writer for two or three years. I was just thinking about the stories I got the most reactions from. One was when the Supreme Court decision came down for Roe v. Wade. Luckily, this fell into my lap. There was a medical group that was going to start an abortion clinic in Fairview Park. I thought, "Oh, great news story."

Even Bill Tanner, who wanted me to write something else at the time, I got him to be less mad at me because I'd come in with a scoop. Man, the calls and letters, the emotional reactions, just for what I thought was a pretty straightforward news story. It was something. There were protests in Fairview Park, and then they never did open there—others opened in the city.

Their protests prompted the city of Cleveland health department to want certain regulations, and the then-head of the Cleveland health department was a man, and as [reporter] Bob Modic put it, "a strong Catholic." So I had to question very carefully, "Is this a personal religious view, or are you really thinking about the health and welfare of your patient?" Because he wanted certain things, like making sure EMS could get in and out of the quarters, and how far do you go in informing, and all that sort of stuff. It was sort of like an unending story. It was my first head-on where you come face to face with true believers, zealots. I was taken aback, and then you have to try to be the usual objective person that holds back your own private, personal views on that. You really wanted to argue with each side, "What are you talking about?"

DARRELL HOLLAND
*Religion Editor,* Plain Dealer

George Plagenz was pretty well known when I got here. For years I'd meet people on the beat and they'd say, "Oh, yeah, you used to rate churches on Sunday mornings." I would say, "No, no, that's George Plagenz at the *Press*." I got tired of doing that, so if they believed it was me, I just let them.

TIM ROGERS

*Sports Reporter,* Press

For an auto supplement, I was assigned to interview Rick Case. I knew nothing about cars. I heard Rick Case only on the radio, advertising, and I thought he was pretty obnoxious. I went there and he showed me some sort of machine to test engines. He said it was the only one in Ohio. So I wrote that—something like "This is the only machine in Ohio that can make your car run like a top." The next day the phone calls started. "Whaddya mean only one in Ohio? There must be 50 of 'em in Ohio. Maybe 50 of 'em in Cleveland." Ah, what did I know? But I didn't check it out.

STU ABBEY

*Reporter, Copy Editor, Editor,* Plain Dealer

A veteran reporter told me, "You always have a story in your pocket for the days that nothing happens."

ROBERT FINN

*Critic,* Plain Dealer

One piece of wisdom I've gleaned over 28 years at the *Plain Dealer* is that if you meet a deadline, the only thing that accomplishes is it brings up the next deadline. There's always another deadline coming along right after the one you just met.

TONY NATALE

*Investigative, General Assignment Reporter,* Press

One of my favorite stories at the *Press* was when I went into the psychiatric ward. I forgot what hospital now. Anyway, I went in there with the help of some nurses or employees. The idea for the story came from a tip we got that something was going on there, that it wasn't being run properly, it was dirty or something. And they let me in and I walked around as a patient just for a day. And I looked around and I saw all of these conditions they were talking about. There were dirty rooms. I saw people in cages, at the time—metal cages, like gorillas, and dirt all over the place. The food wasn't too good either.

I just walked around. I didn't want to be noticed. I just tried to fit in. I didn't act crazy. Again, just to observe. I was there from early in the morning until late in the evening. And they let me out, thank God. I came back and wrote it, and ultimately, I think it was Governor Rhodes, whoever it was—they changed the state laws, certain laws that pertain to state facilities that improved them. I had a sense that I accomplished something.

JIM STRANG
*Reporter,* Plain Dealer

C. Miller Chevrolet used to do all those ridiculous commercials. Well, they ran some kind of a contest where they were going to give away a car to some worthy person. Well, I got this letter from the bureau from a college girl saying she had entered this contest because her father had a heart attack and was disabled and they really needed a car. So they gave her a car, but the car they gave her was a rolling piece of shit. She had two flat tires driving it home; the exhaust system fell off; it was leaking oil; it was just a classic thing. So I talked to her and I talked to her mechanic and talked to the highway patrol, and I called up C. Miller. Well, he just burned the phone line out—f-this, f-that. So I wrote it. And he didn't advertise in the *Plain Dealer* at that point. So he sued me.

That was the first time I had ever been sued. I was sued twice, and this was the first time. The second one was fairly inconsequential. So that's when I first went through the deposition process and all this stuff, sitting down with his lawyer, and the *Plain Dealer* lawyer, and watching the film they show you before you go to the deposition so you don't get to be a smartass and say the wrong thing, and all that stuff. You learn to be very circumspect when you're asked these legal questions. I went through the whole process, and finally the case was just tossed, dismissed with prejudice. Essentially the truth remains a defense. But that was possibly the most rewarding single story I ever wrote, just because the guy was a sham. He had done this thing and I got to tell the world about it. I was good. My stuff was secure.

STEVE TALBOTT
*Reporter,* Plain Dealer

In the early 1980s, mortgage rates were 12 percent and higher. Many older mortgages—with much lower rates—could be assumed by the new buyer under the rules of those days. This made your house much more saleable in a tough market. This loophole was seen by some as a profit opportunity. Rather than just charge processing costs, some S&Ls decided to tack on a big fee and generate some profits. A realtor called and told me about it. So I wrote a Sunday real-estate column about it. The next day I got 40 phone calls. This is a phenomenal response. One or two calls is pretty good. Typical is none. I knew I was on to something.

A couple of weeks later (it took me a while to get it together), I did a story saying that local S&Ls were soaking home buyers. The leading offender was Ohio Savings, which in one case charged more than $3,000 to assume a mortgage in the eastern suburbs. It probably cost them no more than $100 to do the processing. In a couple of months I was able to report that local S&Ls had made refunds totaling something like $90,000. If it was happening in Cleveland, I figured it must be happening elsewhere. I did an FOI to Freddie Mac, the housing finance agency. They said it was personal files and they denied the FOI. It so happened that Mary

Rose Oakar was on the House Banking Committee. I wrote her a letter complaining about Freddie Mac's denial. It also happened that Freddie Mac was before Congress asking for permission to go public—to sell stock. So in a committee hearing, Mary Rose, to her credit and my benefit, put the screws to the head of Freddie Mac. He agreed to supply the documents.

A few weeks later, I got a stack maybe an inch thick showing what Freddie Mac knew about this overcharging and the correspondence it had with various S&Ls about why they were doing it. The stuff showed that Freddie Mac wasn't enforcing its own rule. So over the next couple of months I analyzed the documents and found victims across the country. In August 1983 I did a couple of stories saying that what I had shown was happening in Cleveland was in fact happening "across the country" and that Freddie Mac wasn't enforcing its own rule, which said they could charge processing costs and that's all. A day or two later, Freddie Mac held a news conference in Washington saying it was going to enforce its rule.

It was fun to go to the news conference, but I was so burned out from the series I felt physically ill. In the end, something like 5,000 mortgage holders got refunds totaling more than $2.3 million. On average, it was only a few hundred bucks, but most of these were little people. So I did some good for people. Because of all this, I won some national contests, including a National Press Club "grand prize" for consumer journalism. To get it, I beat out John Stossel of "20/20" on ABC News and Jane Bryant Quinn of the *Washington Post*. And unlike them I didn't have a staff of researchers or producers. I did it by myself—with Mary Rose Oakar's help. It pays to have a congressman on your side. If Mary Rose hadn't been on the banking committee, and if Freddie Mac hadn't been just at that moment standing with its hat in its hand before Congress, I might never have gotten that story, and my life might have been very different. I was damned lucky.

LOU MIO
*Reporter,* Plain Dealer

A lady who was a widow of a World War I veteran lived over in Lakewood and a group of people in Cleveland decided to have a parade for the Vietnam vets that they never had. You might remember this. It was called "Firebase Cleveland." It was a big gathering of Vietnam vets in the city to have a parade. I wrote a story about it. She called and said, "Hi. My name is Carlyn Irwin. And I'm the president of Lakewood Barracks." I said, "What's that?"

Well, it was the World War I equivalent of what became the VFW post and the Legion post. She said, "There's three of us left. And we want to donate our whole treasury to those Vietnam veterans for their parade."

I think there was, like, $32.61. She wrote out the check and sent it along. This was a Page One story. There was the lady with a nice picture of her smiling. When that parade went down Euclid Avenue, she was sitting in a convertible, damn near the grand marshal of that parade. They got her and put her in that parade with her name on the door, and as she went by, people were clapping. They knew who she was from the story.

V. DAVID SARTIN
*Reporter,* Plain Dealer

Early one afternoon an editor came over a bit frantic and gave me a copy of a handwritten letter and he told me, "Hey, you have to read this and see if you can get a story out of it this afternoon."

It was a mother from University Heights who had some hard luck, the family dog was missing and needed medication, and had been missing a couple of days and was probably going to die fairly quickly unless he could get the medication. He was some kind of terrier and his name was Winston. The family dog was best friends to the young boy who was facing his own hurdles. It was a tearjerker. It was a three-hankie job.

My assignment was to find this dog. We knew that dogs were getting picked up and getting euthanized in a few days if they were not claimed by the owners. So I started calling all the pounds around town and I found that dog. The kennel was going to close around 4 o'clock in the afternoon, but the attendant said he would wait around. However, he wanted me to prove it was my dog. Well, it wasn't my dog. It was the kid's dog. So I drove out to the house in University Heights, knocked on the door, the front door was barely ajar and it swung open and there was no answer. But I'm hearing somebody upstairs in the bathroom running water. I'm hearing more sounds. Somebody is in this house. I wait a bit. I'm standing inside the house, I've entered this house, based only on the return address on an envelope. I yell again. It's the mom naked in the bathroom in the tub. I tell her who I am and explained to her that we got her letter and I thought we found the dog.

Now I can't believe this—she actually said, "If you wait a minute, Jimmy"—or Johnny, or whatever his name was—"will be home from school, you can take him to the kennel." She's telling me to take the kid and she's upstairs in the bathroom. I never saw her face. I never saw her. Johnny comes home in about 20 minutes. But she never came downstairs. Can you imagine, would you trust this voice at the bottom of your stairs? So anyway, I get the kid, we go down to the kennel. I get down there and the attendant wants some money. They want the fee. They want the fee they charge to recover the dog. I think it was $17. I had the money in my pocket. I paid the fee. Got the dog. Drove home. To this day, I have never met that woman.

I did get a thank-you note, a tearful thank-you note, and the dog survived. That story didn't amount to beans in a grander scheme of things, but it was front page. It was a helluva story, I had great fun and it was done in the afternoon. I've written stories that caused a cop to resign because he got caught doing bad things, or a mayor to resign, suburban mayor. But somehow finding Winston seems pretty important.

DAN COUGHLIN
*Sportswriter,* Press *and* Plain Dealer

Back in the '70s, a litter of German shepherds was found under a porch and I took one and others took them, too. I would take him out for a walk every night. He got run over. It cost hundreds to put him back together and he no longer looked like a dog. He tail was at an angle and he hopped along on three legs. He didn't really have a name. I called him Brown Fur. I wrote a piece about him after his car accident. It was the first, last, and only story about him. I still can't believe the response from readers—my phone wouldn't stop ringing and the mail was stacked up so high on my desk, it was falling over. They don't teach this in journalism school, but if you're going to write about dogs, get ready to hear from people. A lot of people.

ZINA VISHNEVSKY
*Reporter,* Plain Dealer

I think every reporter hated the dreaded series. A series is nothing more than articles the paper should have published all along, packaged for prize awards. Sometimes it took a year to do a series because the story, which should have been reported all along, kept changing. It was very frustrating to be involved in series projects because you knew that someone was hoping it would get the paper a Pulitzer Prize. Rutti and I spent a year on "At the Crossroads: Catholic Schools in Cleveland." The *PD* really had never covered Catholic education and it was like reinventing the wheel. We never thought that series would see the light of day. It was good work, but could have been published months earlier. Even so, it won a second place in an Associated Press contest. I guess that's all that mattered to some.

BILL TANNER

*Reporter, City Editor,* Press

When I was covering business, the major Cleveland companies were, of course—Republic Steel was one of the big ones, Cleveland Trust was a major force in everything, Jones & Laughlin had a steep couple of years, U.S. Steel. TRW at that time was called Thompson Products, and Fred Crawford was the head of it. He was great as a civic booster. He died at age 97. He was also one of these self-proclaimed [self-]made guys. One time at a civic dinner, he was the master of ceremonies. Louie Seltzer and Frank Coy, the head of the May Company, were sitting next to each other. Fred Crawford looked down at them and said, "I want you to notice that Louie Seltzer and Frank Coy put their heads together and made an ass of themselves."

BOB DANIELS

*Reporter, Rewrite,* Plain Dealer

One time, there was some hanky panky going on in the Wood County auditor's office. I forget exactly what it was. But we were on the story, and I was assigned to it. And so I got on the phone with the auditor in the courthouse and told him who I was and asked him these questions relevant to the story. He was somewhat hesitant. And I said, "I can drive to Toledo and look them up. Why don't you just tell me?" He reluctantly told me what I wanted to know. We talked for five or 10 minutes. And finally I said, "Well, what's your name?" And he said, "I'm not going to tell you." I said, "What do you mean, you're not going to tell me?" And I'd raised my voice a couple of times. By this time there were two or three people standing around my desk. I said, "I can look it up someplace or I can come there or I can call down there and find out what your name is. Why don't you just tell me?" Well, then a few more people started coming around. And I said, "I'm going to really be upset if you persist in not telling me your name. Now what is your name?" And he said something like Prank Jones. I said, "Okay, Prank Jones, what's your middle initial?" He said, "I'm not telling you." Now even more people gathering around. I said, "You've already told me your first name and your last name. Now what's your middle initial?" He said, "I'm not telling you my middle initial." And it's snowing outside. There's basically a low-grade blizzard going on. It was the dead of winter. I said, "Listen pal, if I've got to get in my car and drive to Toledo, Ohio in a blizzard to find out your middle name, you and I are going to have a problem." And bang! I slammed the phone down. And people are clapping. And then it dawned on me, I was talking to a guy in the auditor's office in Toledo, Ohio. The problem was in the Wood County auditor's office in Bowling Green. I was talking to a guy in the wrong county. Not very bright.

# 7.

# Gimme Rewrite, Sweetheart!

### [ THE REWRITE DESK ]

*The rewrite desk had unsung heroes whacking away at keyboards, telephones balanced on their shoulders, listening intently to a reporter's account of a story, questioning the reporters for additional facts. The cacophony that marks a city room went on, as if unconcerned with the rewrite man's work. And work it was. He was responsible for everything that went into the story: names, ages, addresses, all spelled correctly. He needed to know what was done to whom by whom. Time of day, weather and road conditions were vital to some stories; for others, the important details might be caliber of gun, number of shots fired, year and make and model of the getaway car. Once they were satisfied they had gotten all they were going to get from the reporter, the real work started. Rewrite men had to take that jumble of notes and quotes, frame the story with an understanding of the city, and write it in a way that would accurately tell the reader just what the hell happened. It had to be done well and done fast. Slow rewrite men didn't last long. Finally, they attached the reporter's byline to it and took no credit.*

TONY NATALE

*Investigative, General Assignment Reporter,* Press

When I was a copy boy, I was fascinated by some of the rewrite reporters, like Al Ostrow, and Dick McLaughlin, who wrote like Shakespeare. Al Ostrow sat there with his cigarette smoking, while taking notes over the phone and writing stories that just amazed me. He was able to make a story understandable, readable, provide it with flow. Dick McLaughlin was the same, but Mac had a little more artistic touch to his writing. He was a quiet guy with a bowtie and a nice smile. He was very friendly, soft-spoken. I can envision him now with a phone to his ear, hunched over his desk, taking notes with a pencil and, again, putting together Page One stories in a matter of minutes, and as I remember, almost flawless copy.

REED HINMAN
*Sports, Suburban Reporter,* Press

When I was on the state desk, Dick McLaughlin, who was the ace rewrite guy, sat right behind me, and so I was able to observe, when I wasn't busy, some of the ways he handled the job. It was truly amazing. He would be on the phone taking notes—this was before the computers—he'd be taking notes by hand of somebody calling in from the field and asking questions to try to get a feel for what the scene was like, and then he'd hang up and he'd put paper in his typewriter and it would just flow out, and it would be unbelievable. And his name was never on it. It was the reporter's byline on it. He was truly a genius.

ZINA VISHNEVSKY
*Reporter,* Plain Dealer

Reporters, when they called in an unplanned story, were to write it and read it to rewrite with the periods, commas, new grafs, so rewrite could type fast without thinking and think later.

Rewrite also meant writing for Ed Kissell, the longtime night cops reporter who died of a heart attack shortly after retiring to ice skate more or less full-time. Ed was almost a myth. Editors who signed his time sheet had never met him, administration after administration. Ed had a way about him. He would call and start with "I don't know if this is a story . . ." One had better start typing at this point, because he wasn't going to repeat it. Sometimes, it would be a tall tale. But that wouldn't be obvious until the end.

JIM STRANG
*Reporter,* Plain Dealer

E. J. Kissell was a guy we buried without ever knowing where his home was. He lived in an apartment, now Reserve Square on East 12th Street. Once someone from the *Plain Dealer* got on the elevator with him one night and he wouldn't get off. He went up and down a couple of times before the other person finally got off. He never knew what floor E. J. lived on. He was an amazingly private man, but a good reporter.

RICHARD ELLERS
*Reporter,* Plain Dealer

When I started at the *PD*, Bob Daniels was the lead rewrite. He took calls from the police beat, and also did phone interviews. With the big open city room, you could hear the rewrite guys on the phone and Daniels was particularly loud. You could learn reporting, just listening to him.

BOB DANIELS
*Reporter, Rewrite,* Plain Dealer

I think I went to rewrite because when I'd get an assignment to do a story, I'd always get it pretty quickly and cleanly. And for some reason, I've always been a very fast typist. And they needed someone who could write an English sentence, and do so quickly. So I was assigned to rewrite. Probably the best teacher I ever had was when I got to rewrite. That was the late John Depke, who had been on the *Cleveland News* for years. He was on the rewrite desk. And that guy was a reporter. You'd just listen to him work a story. I learned more from him in about six weeks than I had in six years previously.

V. DAVID SARTIN
*Reporter,* Plain Dealer

Rewrite? Yeah, they were good. Sometimes you had to sober them up, but sober they were really good.

STUART ABBEY
*Reporter, Copy Editor, Editor,* Plain Dealer

Adams was on rewrite. The day city editor had a habit of going through the *Press* and *News* and clipping stories for follow-ups. He would write the reporter's name and the length he wanted. Somebody came across a story about a scientist who measured the growth rate of his thumbnails for five years. One of us wrote across it, "Adams, point 5," which meant a half column. A 10-inch story! It was stuck in Adams' mailbox. Believe it or not, Adams does the story, walks up to the city desk and said, "I could only get four-tenths out of this." They also put clips from Chinese newspapers in his mailbox, but he caught on to those pretty quick.

DON BEAN
*Reporter,* Plain Dealer

Bob Daniels was the best rewrite man. He had a flair for writing. He had a flair for accuracy. He had a flair for questioning. One time we almost got into a big fight. Firemen were killed when a battalion chief ordered a dustbin opened and it exploded during a fire in a factory, and Bob Daniels kept insisting that I had to go back and interview that battalion chief to find out why he opened up that dustbin. And I declined to do it. I should have, but I just couldn't do it. I felt bad enough for the guy.

RUSS MUSARRA
*General Assignment Reporter,* Press

I suppose Don Bean was the easiest guy to work with. He was also the most difficult guy to work with because he used to pull tricks on you. But Bean knew what he was doing and he got the job done. I mean, it was just a pleasure to work with him. If you had a question for him, he knew the answer to the question because he had thought to ask it when he was on the story.

I still remember my very first story as a police reporter. Nobody else in the world would remember it, but there was a drowning. A fellow fell or jumped off the East Ninth Street pier and drowned. And I got to the phone first. That's how these things were done. I phoned somebody, got the information, called the city desk, and they gave me to a rewrite man. It was Joe Collier. He was a good writer—a crusty old bastard. I said, "Joe, I got a drowning." He said, "Oh, good." We were supposed to try to dictate the stories as we wanted them to appear in the paper, so I said, "Fred Mertz, 37, of 3684 East 146th Street. He drowned shortly before noon today when he fell off the East Ninth Street pier."

Just as I'm getting to start my second sentence, the rewrite man said, "How deep was the water?" I said, "Well, I don't know." I hear "*click.*" We were disconnected. So I dialed back up and I said, "Excuse me, we were disconnected." He said, "No, we weren't. I hung up on you. Call me back when you've got the details." *Click!* That's how I learned.

DON BEAN
*Reporter,* Plain Dealer

Once, I refused a rewrite man's suggestion—and I got to tell you about this. Fast Eddie Watkins, the bank robber, the famed bank robber that Dick Feagler makes a folk hero out of for his own unknown reasons. But he was a thief and a bank robber, Eddie Watkins. This was 193rd and Lorain, the Cleveland Trust

Bank. I'm trying to think of the year. It had to be '76, '77. I'm not good with dates. But it was before the *Press* went out, of course. Feagler was out there covering it. And Watkins had an explosive device that he said was a bomb, and he went into the bank and he took hostages and he wanted all kinds of money to get out of the country and everything. The idea was to get the hostages out without anybody dying. So they did. But it was quite a long hostage situation. Some wonderful gentleman let the media use his house that was directly across the street from the Cleveland Trust branch. We could watch everything.

Somebody called Mayor Ralph Perk—I think he was running for reelection—and said, "Eddie's about ready to come out." Well, Perk came on the scene. He went into the bank and he came out with Eddie so he could get the exposure on TV, of course.

They took Eddie to Metro Hospital. My job was to go out there and interview him. And I did interview him.

Wagner had gotten him out by promising that he would not be put in a cell, that he would have a room at Metro and so forth and so on. But when he got there, he was put into a prison ward.

The city desk somehow found out about this, and the rewrite man, Joe Campbell, called me at the police beat and said, "Bean, the desk wants you to go to Wagner and asked him why he lied to Watkins." I said, "The city desk wants me to do what?" He repeated it. I said, "Well, it's obvious why he lied to him, if he lied to him. He wanted to get him out without killing anybody. And I'm not going to do that."

So we had a few hot words. Later on that night, I was at the 2300 Club, and I had been there for a while, and Joe Campbell came in. He said, "Bean, what's wrong? Your hemorrhoids hurting you?" And I went up on tippy-toes and I waggled my finger under his nose and I said, "Joe, I'm a perfect asshole. Do you want to check?" He didn't bother to check. I got a little egotistical, I guess.

BOB DANIELS
*Reporter, Rewrite,* Plain Dealer

One time, Bean rang my number directly. And usually you got an assignment on rewrite from the city desk. But the phone rang and it was Bean. And he said, "The desk told me to call you with a funny short. This happened out on Outhwaite Avenue off of East 55th Street. There was a guy by the name of Clarence "Big Jaw" Jackson, age 31 . . . Big Jaw Jackson went down to shoot pool with his buddies tonight."

And he gave the address for the Nickel Plate Pool Room. And he said, "He bet his buddies that he could put the cue ball in his mouth."

"Wait a minute, Bean," I said.

"No, no. Take this down. Take this down."

"All right."

"And so he took the cue ball and he put it in his mouth. And he did it. He won the bet. And then he had this cue ball in this mouth and he said, 'I bet I can put the eight ball in my mouth, too.'"

"Bean, get the hell out of here," I said.

"No, I'm telling you—take this down . . . So, Big Jaw Jackson picked up the eight ball and he got that in his mouth as well. He had the cue ball and the eight ball in his mouth at the same time. And he won that bet. Then, he tried to get them out and he couldn't get them out because they were stuck in his cheeks. And it got to the point where it was impairing his breathing. It was hard for him to breathe. Guys were pushing on his cheeks and on these balls trying to get them out. And they wouldn't come out. So they laid him down on the pool table and they got a Coke out of the Coke machine and they poured it in, trying to lubricate the balls and get them out, and nothing worked. And finally this guy's getting short of breath."

"No shit, Bean," I said. And I'm typing a hundred miles an hour.

Then he said, "It got to the point where they finally had to call the police and they called the rescue squad. And they came and got him."

And I'm taking that down.

"And they put him in the wagon," Bean said, "and they ran him down to Charity Hospital in the emergency room. They put him behind this curtain and an intern came in and one of these guys who are assigned to the emergency room came in and they worked on him for about 10 minutes. They couldn't get the balls out."

And I'm still typing.

"Finally some little student nurse came in," he said. "You know, Daniels, she got those balls out of his mouth like that."

And of course, the brilliant son of a bitch that I am made the mistake of asking, "How'd she do that, Don?"

And he said, "She stuck a cue stick up his ass and knocked 'em out."

My dad used to ask me to tell that story off and on until the day he died. He loved that story—Big Jaw Jackson. After I got done being pissed off, I started laughing. You know, the guy's a genius, to think of something like that. It was very detailed.

# 8.

# "I thought I died and went to heaven."

## [ SPORTSWRITERS ]

*Sportswriters are among journalism's oddities, like mint ice cream in the world of desserts. Sportswriters are not around the office much and have expense accounts. Without charge, they get the best seats in the house and fraternize with the players. They work the most unusual hours, often dress as if they had a signature account at Unique Thrift, and act as if they know everything. The good part is, they do know everything. We read them and quote them. We're eager to argue with them, to show how much we know about the game.*

BOB DOLGAN

*Sports Reporter, Columnist,* Plain Dealer

Did you ever hear about my fight with Sudden Sam McDowell, the Indians pitcher? His first spring training in Tucson was also my first spring training. That was in 1961. Nicknames were still kind of in style in those days. So I'm thinking, "Geez, I gotta come up with something for this guy because this is his first game. It looks like he's going to be great." I just happened to get lucky and thought of Sudden Sam, which is what they still call him today.

A few years later, when I was a publicist at Thistledown racetrack, I went into a crowded bar and McDowell was there, about five seats away from me. We get into an argument and all of a sudden he comes galloping around the bar toward me, looking like he wants to KO me. He was 10 years younger than me and stood 6 feet 6, about 4 inches taller than me. He comes leaping at me, so I closed my eyes and threw two right hands and hit him in the face. And he staggers back like that, and some guys grab him and he goes back to his seat. He wanted to fight some more but I got out of there.

BOB AUGUST
*Sports Editor, Columnist,* Press

I liked former Indians owner Bill Veeck a lot. He was a very interesting man. When Veeck was the owner of the team, I wasn't even in sports. He was gone by the time I was there. But I used to see him around. I can remember the first time I met him and we sat down and talked. And what I always remembered was that he asked my opinion about something. I'm a new guy in the sports department, and that impressed me. Of course, part of this was an act, and I realized it. But that was how he approached the young guys.

I can remember a time that Veeck and I were someplace together and we got to talking. We were both recalling the left-handed pitcher who came up to the Dodgers late in the season and set a record in his first two starts striking out something like 30 or 31 batters. I go back to the office and the phone rings and the phone rings and the voice says, "I remember the pitcher's name." It was Veeck. He was an extraordinary man. He just had a feeling for people.

BURT GRAEFF
*Sports Reporter,* Press

There was a game in San Francisco where Bill Fitch, a couple of assistants and Joe Tait were going from their hotel to the Cow

Palace. Fitch forgot his NBA identification card. At the time, the Cavs were something like 0-15. The security guard was not going to let Fitch into the building because he didn't have his ID with him to show he's an NBA coach. Fitch couldn't believe it and looked at the guy and said, "Do you know what the Cavaliers' record is?" and the guard said, "Yeah, it's something like 0 and 15." Fitch said, "Do you think if I wasn't the coach of the Cavaliers, I'd stand here and admit this to you?" The security guard said, "Go on in."

BOB DOLGAN

*Sports Reporter, Columnist,* Plain Dealer

I never liked Art Modell, because he had been an advertising man from New York, and he came into Cleveland and fired the greatest coach in football, by my standards. Paul Brown had won all these games for 10 years, and he fired him. And I just didn't trust him after that. And I think I turned out to be right. I'm glad. I was virtually his only critic in Cleveland, and I'm glad I criticized him because of the way things turned out. It's the biggest crime against Cleveland sports, I think, ever, pulling the Browns out.

BOB AUGUST

*Sports Editor, Columnist,* Press

It wasn't too many years after Paul Brown became the coach of the Browns that everybody was starting to do the things that he was doing, He just changed everything. Paul had a lot of the characteristics of coaches. He had paranoia. In some of his dealings with people, he could be very, very mean. But he also had qualities that you admired. He was an extraordinary executive and leader, at that time. I was covering him when he was right at the peak of his career. I think after that, Paul was always a good football coach, but he had lost that enormous advantage that he once had by doing so many things that nobody else did.

BOB YONKERS

*Reporter, Editor, Assistant to Editor,* Press

Paul Brown was a Jekyll and Hyde. He was tough on his players, very much a disciplinarian. But he was very sociable off the field. I never had any problems with him, except one time when we had a story in the paper—this was in the All-American conference when the Browns and 49ers were the top teams—and they were going to play the Brooklyn Dodgers, and the 49ers were playing the New York Yankees. The headline says, "Tough One for Browns, Soft Touch for 49ers." I didn't write that. They beat the Brooklyn Dodgers, I think 7-6. And I had been delayed in the press box getting statistics. We went down in the dressing room and reporters are surrounding Brown. He points and says, "Your fault, Yonkers." I said, "What did I do? You didn't even dress me for the game." That broke him up.

DAN COUGHLIN

*Sportswriter,* Press *and* Plain Dealer

He was a warrior without a war. That was Woody Hayes. I never spent any time with him until 1981. He was sick and out of coaching. He had his gallbladder taken out and they had to open him a second time to retrieve medical tools they forgot. He had lost a great deal of weight. But I spent a whole day with him and was so inspired by him, I wrote the longest—and probably the best—newspaper story I ever wrote.

His office was on the second floor of the ROTC building. He had to give a talk at the Kiwanis and he drove like a madman. When we got back, I wanted to help him up the stairs, but that just pissed him off. Anyway, we talked the whole day. He was incredibly honest. He had served on a destroyer in World War II. He had theories for this and that. Woody rubbed a lot of people the wrong way with his honesty, but after that day, he became one of my all-time favorite people.

BOB DOLGAN

*Sports Reporter, Columnist,* Plain Dealer

In the 1980s, I was at a Browns game and I noticed that some of the players, when they'd make a tackle, they'd lean over the guy and it looked as if they were yelling. Nobody knew what the hell they were doing. So the next day, I asked Hanford Dixon, the defensive back who was kind of the leader of the defense.

"We're barking," he said.

"What do you mean, 'barking?'" I asked

"We were going, 'woof, woof.'"

"For what?"

"Well, we just want to do it. Our whole defense is doing that. It kind of gives us a good attitude. We're all together and we're barking."

So I wrote a column on that and that led to the Dawg Pound. I admit, I did not think of the Dawg Pound. And I did not spell it "d-a-w-g." I spelled it "d-o-g." Nevertheless, it was the first time that there was a story on the Dawgs, and that took root after that game.


REED HINMAN

*Sports, Suburban Reporter,* Press

Alvin Dark was the Indians manager, and had just gotten married. An editor calls me and says, "Dark's wife is from New York and she's at the game, so go find her." We found where she was sitting and I went over there and talked to her. Then I went into the pressroom at Yankee Stadium to eat. Russ Schneider, the *Plain Dealer* baseball writer, is there and I said, "Is that Joe DiMaggio over there?" He said, "Hell, yeah, that's Joe DiMaggio over there." So this is pretty heavy stuff for a guy—I was twentysomething. So I got the sidebar with Alvin Dark's wife and I think that worked out okay. Then I wrote a story about the game. I wrote that the Indians center field played with aplomb. Boy, did I hear about that when I got back to Cleveland. Jerry Kvet comes up to me and he says, "'Aplomb'—I never heard of that word."

BURT GRAEFF
*Sports Reporter,* Press

When I was hired, I told my girlfriend I was moving to Cleveland and she said she was going with me. We were driving through a small town in Georgia and saw this banner: "Get Married For $22," so I asked her if she wanted to get married. The justice of the peace was also the guy who ran the gas station. We went to his house and his wife turned out to be the witness. I was wearing jeans and T-shirt and my girlfriend was wearing a muumuu. In the other room was a TV with a baseball game on and the justice of the peace told his wife to turn it off. My girlfriend said, "No, he's a sportswriter. Leave it on." The Dodgers were playing the Reds. Twenty-two bucks and the marriage lasted 10 years, so I thought it was a pretty good investment.

BOB DOLGAN
*Sports Reporter, Columnist,* Plain Dealer

Gene Green was an outfielder with the Indians, a big strong guy, good hitter, terrible fielder. He would've been a perfect DH, but they didn't have DHs at that time. And he liked to go out on the town. There were always about seven guys on the team that liked to carouse a little bit, and he was one of them, and he was great at it. So I knew him fairly well. And one day we're flying from Los Angeles to Washington. We were about halfway across the country, and I'm sitting next to Jerry Kindall, the second baseman, on the plane. I used to just look around the plane to make sure everybody was on the plane, and I didn't see Green. So I said to Birdie Tebbetts, who was managing that year, "Birdie, where's Gene Green?" He said, "I don't know, and I don't give a damn." So I told Kindall, "If we get to Washington and we haven't heard from Green, I'm going to write a story saying that he jumped the team." Kindall said, "That's preposterous" So we get to Washington and we didn't hear from Green, but I knew where he hung out. So I called the bar and I said, "Hello. Is Gene Green there?" And the bartender said, "Hold on a minute." And Green comes to the phone. I said, "Gene, what the hell are you doing there? We're in Washington! What are you doing in L.A.?" He said, "The hell with those guys. I'm quitting baseball. I'm through with them. I'm sick of all of them." He was mad because he wasn't playing every day. And he tells me all this stuff. That was a good scoop. I was the only guy who knew where Gene Green was. Even Gabe Paul and Tebbetts didn't know where he was. It was a real good story. Of course, the next day he showed up and forgot everything.

BOB AUGUST

*Sports Editor, Columnist,* Press

I remember Ernie Davis. He was the Heisman Trophy winner out of Syracuse and broke the team's records. I got close to Ernie. I did a piece for *The Saturday Evening Post* on Ernie after he found out he had leukemia. So I spent plenty of time with him. The Browns had just played a game, and Jim Brown had done something, one of those amazing things he did, and I said to Ernie, "Ernie, could you do things like that?" Because people said that this guy was as good as Jim Brown. And he just laughed and said, "You know, I'm not half that strong."

BOB DOLGAN

*Sports Reporter, Columnist,* Plain Dealer

Probably the column that I wrote that I got the most response on was a piece on Don Rogers, the Browns defensive back. He died of a cocaine overdose the day before his wedding, in the '80s. He was a damn good player, nice guy, too. I found that people who are cocaine addicts all have great personalities, every one I've ever talked to. You see a guy in a corner who's bitching about something, grouchy—they never use cocaine. It's always the guys who are the nicest guys on the team. So anyway, he died of a cocaine overdose, and there was some talk about having a moment of silence for him before the first Browns game, or playing the season with a black armband or something like that. And I wrote a column saying that I didn't think it was a good idea because, to me, what he did was really stupid. Why glorify him?

Then I went into a lot of details about his lifestyle. He wasn't marrying the mother of his child. He was marrying another woman. I said, "Why didn't he marry her?" And he bought his brother, who just got out of college, a $30,000 car. And I said something like "What's wrong with a $6,000 car?" which would've been expensive at that time. Why did he have to buy a $30,000 car? Well, the mail poured in more than I had ever seen. There was no e-mail in those days, everything was written. I was getting phone calls. Every day they'd bring me a stack of mail this high. I got about a thousand letters and calls. And for weeks, I'd be walking down the street and somebody would stop the car and say, "Hey, Bob." I said, "I know. I know what you're gonna say." They liked the column. It was amazing. I'd never gone through anything like that before or since. I wonder how much I would've gotten if e-mail was around in those days.

BRENT LARKIN

*Politics,* Press

I majored in journalism because I wanted to be a sports editor. I wanted to be a sportswriter and then a sports editor. And as my career progressed, I had a couple of chances to do that, but I went down a different path that I don't regret at all. But I'm a sports nut. My whole life I have been. And when I was at OU, when I was sober, I did a couple internships for the *Athens Messenger* where I covered high school football. So that's what I wanted to do. I wanted to be a sportswriter.

TIM ROGERS

*Sports Reporter,* Press

I went from being a drummer in a two-bit rock-and-roll band to a guy with two weeks on the job, and Nate Wallach, the Browns' PR guy, walks in, throws down this big envelope on my desk and says, "Okay, sonny, here's your season tickets. Don't ask for any more." Inside, 16 tickets to the Browns games. Forty-yard line, upper deck. I thought I died and went to heaven.

BURT GRAEFF

*Sports Reporter,* Press

You would go to the Western Union office to send in your story. I enjoyed it because I was young and going to places I'd never been to. Before I'd go, I'd read about the cities. I tried to take advantage of places, like museums. I loved walking around talking with people . . . Boston, Chicago, New York, the West Coast. I tried to take as much advantage as I could because I didn't know if I would ever get back to these places. I liked going on the road until one time I woke up and didn't know where I was. I was at home.

BOB DOLGAN

*Sports Reporter, Columnist,* Plain Dealer

In my first year on the beat, in 1961, the Indians took a bus from Chicago to Minnesota. Jimmy Dykes was the manager. I was the only writer there. I don't know why the other two guys weren't there. It was an off day. We pulled up to a restaurant and Dykes says, "Okay, let's stop here and go out and get a sandwich."

We all got out, ate and came back on the bus. But Vic Power, the Gold Glove first baseman, was missing. Dykes says, "Where the hell's Power?" After a minute or so, Power ambled back. Dykes, who was about 65 then, was so furious he suddenly looked bigger, stronger and younger than Power. He screamed at Power, "Where were you, you son of a bitch?" And Power says, "I didn't know I was supposed to be back here. You didn't tell us what time we had to be back." Power was a real nice guy. Dykes was screaming at him and I'm sitting there, the only newspaperman on the bus.

Now that would've made a hell of a story, wouldn't it? But I blew it. I was so concerned with these guys all telling me "you print everything you hear." I wanted to show them that I could keep a confidence. Since there was no other writer on the bus I never wrote the story, which was really stupid because the other two reporters who were not there could've heard it from somebody else and I would have been scooped on my own story. Fortunately, they never heard about it.

Lesson learned. A few years later, the Indians had a relief pitcher named Fred Funk. They announced during a game that they were going to send him down to the minors. I went and talked to him, along with the other writers. And he's blowing his stack at the manager, Mel McGaha. I was asking questions and taking notes right in front of him. It was a hell of a story. It was a better story than the ballgame. They ran it on the top. That night, Funk gets scared. I guess he saw the first edition. It was a daytime game. So he must've seen the first edition or somebody told him. And he calls the TV station and denies everything that he said. So the next day, Cobbledick calls me and he says, "Bob, Funk says he never talked to you." I said, "Cobby, everything he said is in there, word for word. That's exactly the way he said it." And Cobbledick said, "OK. That's good enough for me." Three weeks later the Indians recalled Funk from the minors. I saw him in a bar and asked him why he denied complaining to me. He said, "Geez, I didn't know you were going to quote me."

The *Cleveland Press* building at Lakeside and East 9th opened in 1959. "It was spotless," said reporter Harriet Peters. "Louis Seltzer would go up and down the aisles, bending over, picking up all the scraps of paper. *(Cleveland Press Collection, Cleveland State University Archives)*

September 8, 1954. *Plain Dealer* building at the northwest corner of E. 6th Street and Superior Avenue. *(The Plain Dealer)*

Louis B. Seltzer became editor of the *Press* at the age of 28 and led the paper for almost 40 years. Helen Moise: "The *Press* had more of a connection with the community because number one with Louie Seltzer was that you answer your phone when it rings. And we did." *(CSU)*

*Plain Dealer* publisher and editor Thomas Vail came from money and didn't seem comfortable with his employees. His style couldn't have been more different from that of Louis Seltzer. *(CSU)*

*Press* copydesk, 1978. "A patient at a psychiatric hospital would come in at least once a week," said Dick Feagler. "He would perch on the rim of the copy desk and just sit there. We thought he blended very well with the copy editors." *(CSU)*

*Plain Dealer* city room, 1964. The city room was command headquarters for coverage of the entire city and beyond. No industry or business ever had the choreographed chaos and daily success of a newspaper city room. *(The Plain Dealer)*

When John F. Kennedy was shot, the country was in shock, but newsrooms (as pictured here at the *Press*) were humming, and the bells on the teletype machines were ringing. *(CSU)*

"With the two newspapers, you were always trying to outdo the other," said Wally Guenther (center), an investigative and general assignment reporter for the *Press*. Here he jogs with Chagrin Falls housewives. He also infiltrated the Ku Klux Klan. *(CSU)*

*Press* photographer Tony Tomsic did whatever it took to get the shot. He was also one of the first newspaper photographers in town to start using a 35mm camera. *(CSU)*

Bus Bergen of the *Press* was a legendary reporter with a sense of humor. He stuck with his manual typewriter. "Bergen could not, would not, did not want to go anywhere near one of these IBM Selectrics," said Tom Skoch. *(CSU)*

Brent Larkin (center): "The greatest local politician I covered was George Forbes (far left). He was the master of understanding power and the use of power." Also pictured are *Press* executive editor Herb Kamm (far right) and city editor Bill Tanner (foreground). *(CSU)*

Mayor Carl B. Stokes (left) faces the *Plain Dealer*'s James Naughton, Robert McGruder and Bill Barnard. March 4, 1969. *(The Plain Dealer)*

The police beat wasn't easy, but with criminals like Danny Greene and Shondor Birns to cover, it wasn't boring, either. Many young reporters, like the *Press*'s Jim Marino, started out on the police beat before moving on to other positions. *(CSU)*

Mayor Ralph Perk pays a visit to the city desk in the *Press* office. Dick Feagler said, "The joke used to be that there was a tunnel from the *Press* to city hall and Louie Seltzer pulls the strings." *(CSU)*

Both papers had a religion writers; the *Plain Dealer* also had a Catholic writer. Here, *Press* religion writer George Plagenz is being interviewed by CBS. *(CSU)*

*Press* photographers Fred Bottomer (seated center) and (clockwise) Herman
Seid, Larry Nighswander, Van Dillard, Tim Culek, Frank Reed, Tony Tomsic, Paul
Toppelstein, Bernie Noble, Bill Nehez, Clayton Knipper, Paul Tepley, 1974. *(CSU)*

A "double masthead" edition, with both the *Press*'s and the *Plain Dealer*'s names, ran during a three-day strike by truck drivers. May 18, 1972. *(CSU)*

*Press* city room. *(CSU)*

Checking copy at the *Press*. Tony Tucci (left), Betty Klaric and Hil Black, 1977. *(CSU)*

Doris O'Donnell: "My mother said, 'You're never going to be a newspaper reporter. You have to be a secretary like your cousins.'" *(The Plain Dealer)*

Reporters like Barbara Weiss at the *Press* covered almost everything in their careers, from the home magazine to the police beat, engagements and obits. *(CSU)*

Dick Feagler getting the story in 1976. He was a reporter for the *Press* before he became a columnist. *(CSU)*

A corner of the *Press* women's department with Darlene Johnson (left) and Rusty Brown in the foreground and Women's Editor Pat Rueter (seated) and Foods Editor Barbara Bratel. May 11, 1977. *(CSU)*

The *Plain Dealer* coming off the press. *(Cleveland Public Library)*

*Plain Dealer* newsroom, election night, 1965. *(The Plain Dealer)*

*Press* editorial department, 1979. "The biggest shock when technology started coming was how quiet everything got," said Tom Skoch. "The silence was disturbing." *(CSU)*

*Press* reporter Teddi Gibson-Bianchi with an audiologist, covering the release of the movie "Earthquake" in January, 1975. *(CSU)*

"I broke a lot of stories in the suburbs," said Brent Larkin. "I developed a lot of sources. I liked to work the phones." Larkin moved to the *Plain Dealer* shortly before the *Press* was shut down. *(CSU)*

Papers roll from the conveyor that leads from the pressroom to the mailroom of the *Press* building at E. Ninth Street and Lakeside Avenue. From here, it was on to the delivery trucks, the paperboys, and your front door. *(CSU)*

TONY TOMSIC

*Photographer,* Press

    The Super Bowl I remember the most is the Namath Super Bowl. That's the one he predicted they were going to win, and they were 18-point underdogs. I remember because it was one of the dumbest games of my life. I was being super-stubborn, and I made up my mind before the game—we all had little game plans—I was going to get a picture of Joe Namath getting sacked. So I stayed behind him for the whole game, to the bitter end I stayed. I never got that picture. I did run behind him with his arms in the air. Of course, I missed a lot of pictures because the offense was going in the opposite direction. I figured I was going to get that picture. I saw all the other guys going the other way, but I held my ground, and I paid the price.

BOB DOLGAN

*Sports Reporter, Columnist,* Plain Dealer

    When I was writing baseball, there was a catcher named Jose Azcue. This was in the early '60s. He was a nondescript player that the Indians got from Kansas City on a trade for Dick Howser. Azcue turned out to be a very personable guy, a good Joe, but he was on the bench most of the time. I think he started playing because John Romano, who still has the Indians record for most homers in a season, was hurt. Azcue started making a bunch of clutch hits. For about two or three weeks, he kept getting all these hits, winning ballgames. So I called him, "The Immortal Joe Azcue." The last story about the Immortal Joe Azcue was on the day before the All-Star game in Cleveland. All the writers came into Cleveland for the game. That was in 1963. This veteran writer for the United Press International—he was the sports editor of the UPI—objected to me calling Azcue, "The Immortal." He was a very serious baseball man. He said, "The only immortals are people like Lou Gehrig, Babe Ruth, Ted Williams—people like that, not a guy like Joe Azcue." I couldn't believe he missed the point.

BOB AUGUST
*Sports Editor, Columnist,* Press

In '64, I started to write about the Indians when I was a columnist. All those years, they had a few very good players, but they never had enough of them. It was a frustrating experience. They never even got close to doing anything important during those years. But I enjoyed it.

TIM ROGERS
*Sports Reporter,* Press

Covering a game? Well, it's not rocket science.

BOB DOLGAN
*Sports Reporter, Columnist,* Plain Dealer.

Sports Editor Hal Lebowitz was good to work for. He was good if you had feature stories. He loved feature stories. He didn't waste much time either. Today they have meetings. But then, you'd say, "Hal, I have this story. I talked to this guy." He'd say, "Good, good. Let me have it."

REED HINMAN
*Sports, Suburban Reporter,* Press

I was sent down to the stadium to do a sidebar. In those days, we would always send two people down. Bob Sudyk would write the game story, and another person was there to look for the color story. The Indians were playing the Washington Senators and the Indians were behind 8 to nothing, or something like that, going into the last of the ninth inning. Then they came back and they had narrowed the score—they had the bases loaded, two outs, and Washington calls in a relief pitcher. The guy gives up a grand slam and the Indians win the game, 9-8, or 10-9.

Sudyk says, "Go down to the Washington locker room and talk to that pitcher." It was the first time I'd been in a locker room, especially the visiting team's locker room. They don't know me, and I don't know what to do there. So I find who this pitcher was. He was sitting there half undressed, and everyone's cussing and whatever. So I go up to the guy and I introduced myself, and I said, "So that was sort of a difficult situation. I mean, what pitch did you throw?" The next thing I know, there's this beer can flying right past my head. I went back and I told the sports editor, "I'm outta here. I'm not doing this sports stuff anymore. This is bullshit. These guys are all overpaid assholes." I got moved to what we called the state desk.

BOB DOLGAN

*Sports Reporter, Columnist,* Plain Dealer

In 1961 Harry Jones surprised everybody. He quit as the *Plain Dealer* baseball writer. Everybody thought he'd be the next sports editor. That was how the *PD* usually operated. When a sports editor retired, the baseball writer would succeed him. Jones had been on the beat 13 years. I asked him, "Why'd you quit, Harry?" He said, "I can't stand the thought of writing another word."

# 9.

# "I got so many calls about Liberace . . ."

## [ CRITICS ]

*One of many roles filled by newspapers was criticism: restaurants, films, theater, music of all sorts. If critics were going to be of service to readers, they had to know the difference between al dente and alfresco, "The Magnificent Ambersons" and "The Godfather," stage right and stage left, strings and woodwinds. A good critic, one with a solid foundation in his or her art, wrote interesting copy. It was, after all, written from a unique perspective. Perhaps best of all, their copy was the stuff of wonderful debate; among readers, there were men and women who knew more about the subject than the critic.*

TEDDI GIBSON-BIANCHI

*Entertainment Critic, Medical Reporter,* Press

Frequently you don't know what kind of response you're going to get from a reader. I wrote a somewhat critical review of Liberace at the Front Row. Well, his fans were not happy with me. The only other story I remember getting as much response from was on abortion. Oh, man, I got so many calls about Liberace. So many ladies were so mad at me because I said he was pounding on the piano. And Tony Mastroianni said, "Don't worry, that happened to me when I said it was more of a fashion show."

FRANK HRUBY
*Music Critic,* Press

After the war, I got a job teaching composition and theory and all those good things at Mississippi Southern College in Hatties-burg, Miss. I went down there and when they saw my résumé they said, "Oh, you'd be a good one to write music reviews for the *Hattiesburg American."* It was a paper that came out once a week. My pay was three tickets to the concerts. They had really big names that would come for one-night stands. They had four major programs a year. And the president of the college, who was on the concerts board, suggested I write the reviews. It went fine for one year, and into my second year, duo pianists put on a performance that I reviewed, and I thought they had played a very routine concert. They just played, picked up their checks, and left. So I reported that.

The next day, I was out in front of our little cottage on campus and the president drove by and said, "Mr. Hruby, I have a little question about your review of that concert last night. You were kind of rough on them, weren't you?"

"Well, those are famous pianists," I said, "and I think, no matter what the audience thought or what the background of the people listening is, or the musical experience, the artists should do their best. And I just don't feel that they did."

"Well, you know," he said, "the board appreciates your efforts, but they feel that you don't need to do the rest of it for the year." So that was the end of that. But I saved all those reviews in a little book that I got at the dime store, and pasted them in, like a fledgling journalist.

ROBERT FINN
*Critic,* Plain Dealer

I was to review a recital by the great Canadian contralto Maureen Forrester, who was singing in the Cleveland Chamber Music

Society, and I came home mid-afternoon and I said to my wife, "I feel terrible. My nose is running. I have a headache. I think I have a temperature. I feel miserable." She said, "Why don't you get somebody else to review the concert, and just stay home. You're in no fit condition." I said, "Listen, if listening to Maureen Forrester singing Robert Schumann's 'Mondnacht' can't cure me, then I'm hopeless. It's the end of the world." "Mondnacht" is a song by Robert Schumann whose title means "dedication." It's one of his great songs. And she was going to sing a group of Schumann's songs, including that song. It was just a song that I loved. So I dragged myself to the concert, and do you know, by the time that concert was over, I felt fine. And I've always felt that there's a therapeutic power in music that can do that. I can't explain it. I don't understand it. I don't know why it happened, but it happened. I felt fine when that concert was over.

DIANA MCNEES

*Photographer,* Plain Dealer

I was in New York, shooting fashion for Janet McCue. She was mis-assigned. She should have been the travel editor. She knew how to find the greatest little places, good restaurants and bars. When she wrote about the places, she was funny. So I could never figure out why she went into fashion. There's nothing funny about fashion. It's grueling, it's stupid and it's ridiculous.

HARRIET PETERS

*Television Reporter,* Press

Louis Seltzer almost fired me when I was in the radio/TV department, which is where I went as an assistant after being copy boy. In those days, we would call NBC in New York every day to get the guests for the "Tonight Show" so that we would have the most current listings in our TV previews. That was one thing that I was in charge of. I misunderstood over the telephone the description of one of the guests, as I wasn't familiar with his name. I had him listed in the paper as So-and-So Racketeer. Well! Probably nobody would have noticed that, much less Louis, because the previews were probably in 6-point or 4-point type, but this particular gentleman that I called a racketeer was scheduled to speak or lecture at John Carroll University and he was a *raconteur,* not a racketeer. One of the priests at John Carroll called Louis Seltzer ranting and raving, so Louis came ranting and raving to me and, of course, we printed a big apology, which was fine with me, but I'll never forget. I should have had some sense, but Johnny Carson and the "Tonight Show" had some very unusual guests.

ROBERT FINN
*Critic,* Plain Dealer

There are ways to be critical. The way I always put it is, you don't have to call a spade a shovel. There are ways to say things where you can say what you have to say without necessarily being nasty about it, or trampling on somebody's self-respect. Once or twice, I simply called the desk and I said, "Look, this concert is really bad. It's not worth wasting paper on, wasting our space on. Let's just forget the whole thing."

FRANK HRUBY
*Music Critic,* Press

Louie Seltzer said, "Well, it's not much of a job. You're only out two times a month, maybe. But would you like it?" Well, I knew it was more than that. The Cleveland Orchestra played every week, and there were other concerts. So I said, "Yes, I would like to give it a try." He said, "I'll turn you over to Jim Frankel and we'll see what we can do."

It was summertime and the Cleveland Pops Orchestra was performing—that was in 1956—and it was Cole Porter night that particular evening that we had in mind. Jim said, "I have two tickets. Come along and you sit there and review the concert, then I'll take you back to the *Press*. I have a lot of work I can do. I'll sit there while you write the review, and we'll put it in the paper and see how it goes, see if Louie likes it." That was fine with me. Well, I had done three Cole Porter shows at Cain Park so I was very well acquainted with his music and what he stood for. I wrote the review and handed it to Jim. I did it in about 45 minutes, which was fast, even for me later on. I said, "Okay, Jim, here it is." He had a stack of books that he was going to read while I struggled all night with this review.

ROBERT FINN

*Critic,* Plain Dealer

Frank Hruby and I got along very well. We never sat together, maybe by accident once or twice, but Frank and I are still friends. He's a member of one of the great musical families, of course. At one time I think there were five people named Hruby playing in the Cleveland Orchestra. Frank was a clarinetist and a conductor. He was a conductor of the Singers' Club for many years. And he treated me as a colleague. We were competitive, of course, certainly, but there was this fellow feeling between the two of us because we both love music and we wanted our readers to love music, too.

FRANK HRUBY

*Music Critic,* Press

When we did reviews, we rarely traveled with the orchestra because the *Press* never wanted to sponsor to that degree. Most of the time, when a critic accompanies the orchestra, he stays the whole time the orchestra stays and attends all the concerts. That makes sense. But if the *Press* editors didn't approve, they would say, "Well, go to a couple of concerts, and then come back." For instance, on their famous tour where they sort of broke the Iron Curtain—remember that? It was one of the first major music organizations to go to the Soviet Union. It was very successful. But I wasn't included.

The orchestra started in Russia, then they were scheduled to hit the four Scandinavian countries. Well, the PR people for the Scandinavian countries called me up and said, "Mr. Hruby, would you like to come review the Cleveland Orchestra in all four countries on their upcoming tour?"

I had to check with the *Press.* I went to Louie and said, "How about it?"

"Fine," he said. "I'll give you 200 bucks to help you along the way."

The Scandinavians sent me a round-trip ticket. I would be four days in Finland, Sweden, Norway and Denmark. It was all taken care of. That was my first trip overseas since the war. It had to be exactly four days because all four countries were footing the bills. So I couldn't be five days in one and three in another. And they arranged the whole itinerary. They had arranged their music festivals that they have every year, one after the other, so the Cleveland Orchestra could perform at each one. The orchestra was received marvelously. There were full houses, big spreads in the newspapers. I felt like an ambassador of music—it's one of the best jobs.

ROBERT FINN
*Critic,* Plain Dealer

I would say that the Cleveland audience was not the most sophisticated audience in the United States. There were a lot of fine professional musicians in town, but the general audience tended to be interested in names rather than music. In other words, if there was a big name coming to town, that's what would draw them. And I'm afraid this is still true. One of the things I tried to do in my 28 years at the *Plain Dealer* was to upgrade the level of musical sophistication in this town, by trying to show people, look, there's something going on over here, maybe in some church basement or something, that you would find interesting if you would go. You might find that you like this. And to try to get them interested in things other than the big name coming to town with the Metropolitan Opera or a soloist with the Cleveland Orchestra, or in the Oberlin recital series, or what have you. It's not always a big name that makes great music.

BILL BARNARD
*Reporter, Editor,* Plain Dealer

When I was a copy boy, the city editor, assigned me to Herbert Elwell, who covered the Orchestra. He would come in from covering a concert, he and his wife. He would wear a tuxedo and she would be dressed in a gown. Both of them had some sherry, or something, in between. He would sit at the typewriter and fall asleep. She would be dozing. In those days copy boys made "books," which were three pages of copy paper and we'd put two pages of carbon paper between them. When he would fall asleep, I'd take it out of his typewriter and put another one in and he'd go back to typing.

HARRIET PETERS
*Television Reporter,* Press

Bruno Bornino, who was in charge of reviewing records and rock concerts and other kinds of popular music concerts, he just loved his job. He happened to be sitting at a desk near mine, he was on the telephone and he hangs up the telephone and turns to look at us in the entertainment area and he says, "the King is dead," and it was Elvis who died. This was a very sad moment for Bruno.

# 10.

# More Than a Snapshot

## [ PHOTOGRAPHERS ]

*Let's get one thing straight: The* Press *and* Plain Dealer *photographers had about as much to do with paparazzi as the American Legion did with Legionnaires' Disease. And while digital cameras allow more pictures to be taken today, it hardly means the pictures will be better.*

*What an unusual job was newspaper photography. The photographers were charged with showing us at our very best and our very worst. Leading the St. Patrick's Day parade or being paraded off to prison. On many stories, the guy with the big Speed Graphic camera wasn't welcome.*

*The job was anything but routine. Photographers wanted much more than a snapshot; they wanted a picture that revealed more than it disguised, a black-and-white image that would add immeasurably to the story. By and large, photographers were just as creative, just as inventive and just as much fun as reporters.*

PAUL TEPLEY

*Sports Photographer,* Press

Back then, there was a strange way that guys got to be photographers. They didn't go to school. Most of them didn't have training. I'm talking about the older guys. Clayton Knipper was one of them. He worked for a newspaper as a copy boy or something, and someone said, "Why don't you become a photographer?" It was a different way. There was no formal way of learning photography. I don't know if they're natural. I think you kind of get better as you work at it. I'm sure good photographers see things that other people don't see and they're able to transmit that. Trying to describe what photographers are like now and describing photographers back in the Speed Graphic days are two different things. You put a film holder in the camera and cock the shutter and focus manually, and you guess-focus mostly. It's not like picking up a 35-millimeter camera and shooting 36 pictures in the time you could've gotten two pictures with the Speed Graphic. So it was a more disciplined thing. You really made sure you waited for just the right moment to shoot a picture because if you didn't, you couldn't recover. It was very much more demanding.

DIANA MCNEES

*Photographer,* Plain Dealer

I had done my internship for Kent State at the *Press* in 1973. I worked for Clayton Knipper. I didn't know how to use a strobe when I went there. Kent State had a couple of professors who said, "Well, when the sun goes down, put the camera away," that sort of thinking. Knipper saw that I couldn't use a strobe. He was going on vacation. He said, "I'm going on vacation for two weeks. When I come back, if you don't know how to use a strobe, you're outta here." I learned.

DICK FEAGLER

*Reporter, Columnist,* Press

I was with Clayton Knipper and we were trying to get an interview with somebody. It was out around Norwalk and there was a crime involved. I went up to the door and knocked. Nobody came to the door. I knocked again and nobody came to the door.

So I said to Clayton—this was before we had car phones or cell phones—"Well, I suppose we could go up by the drugstore and call him and see if he'll answer the phone." And Clayton says, "No. You don't know how to knock on the door. I'll show you how to knock on the door." He starts beating on this door constantly, and he's keeping up this conversation while he's doing this, "They can stay in there, and they can ignore it, but they're only going to do that for so long. Pretty soon this is going to annoy the hell out of them and they're not going to be able to stand it anymore and they're going to come and they're going to open the door." And they did. So now I know how to knock on a door. It's kind of hard on your hand.

TONY TOMSIC
*Photographer,* Press

We used a Speed Graphic—it's a big press camera that you see in the old movies of the '30s and the '40s. The piece of film was 4x5 inches, and you put that in on a plate on the back of the camera. So imagine 4x5 inches. The picture you get in the drugstore today is 4x6, so the film itself was that big. I was one of the first guys at the *Press* to use a 35-millimeter.

The society of engineers held an annual industrial fair for students. They were going to do the whole feature page opposite the editorial page. It amounted to a picture page, usually about six to eight pictures. And I got the assignment. It's kind of a dry assignment because you got a bunch of people standing around. There's nothing to it, there are no bouncing balls; there's charts and people standing and looking at things. And they made a point of telling me to try and do something different with it.

Of course, with the *Press* camera you had to use a big flash and everything. I took the 35-millimeter camera there. I thought what I did was a pretty good job. I brought the pictures in and the managing editor then, Dick Campbell, read the riot act to

me, and was really pissed at the pictures. They were grainy. We
didn't have anything else and I remember he chewed me out
early in the morning.

Then he saw the layout. I get a phone call, and I'll tell you,
it was hard for this guy. He called me in his office. He says, 'Sit
down!" I'll never forget that. Then he sits down. I moved and he
says, "Sit back!" I said, 'I'm not going to sit back!" I got pissed.
Then he says, "I was wrong. You were right. This looks pretty
damn good." So we started to use it a little bit more then. The
pictures were great in there, but at the time, with the printing
presses and everything, they looked a little bit different. And I
started using the 35 more and more. The newspaper would've
gone to the 35 whether I did it or not. I remember going back to
the darkroom and a couple of guys said to me, "I knew that would
happen. I knew that would happen and I'm glad it was you."

FRANK ALEKSANDROWICZ
*Photographer,* Press

I went to shoot some vandalism in Euclid. It was at the high
school. I was coming back to the newspaper on the Shoreway.
I was pressing on the accelerator, not paying attention to the
speed limit. I heard a siren and saw the police car behind me.
The officer says, "What's your hurry?" I said, "I'm on a deadline."
He says, "Well, you're dead now." Somebody at the *Press* made
arrangements that I'd be the first one on the docket. The judge
gave me a speech. He added, "Louie Seltzer would not be happy
with your driving."

TONY TOMSIC
*Photographer,* Press

The Sleeping Beauty sisters—the mother who drugged her
two sleeping daughters, if you remember that. Bill Tanner and I
got into trouble at the trial in 1960. This was in the juvenile court

and during a recess, Tanner took some evidence off of the table. The evidence hadn't been presented yet. I was told about this, and in a side room, I photographed it. But what Tanner didn't know was that the husband happened to be sitting in the court- room and evidently he saw Tanner take it. We got caught. Bill was outside. The Inner Belt was just being constructed and they had to rebuild the sidewalk in front of the criminal courts building. I had come in the side door. I had the camera in my left hand. I had the film—it was a 4x5 *Press* camera, so they were big plates—and as I'm going out the door, charging down the stairs, this guy had just gotten finished putting in the sidewalk and I'm going full tilt. And it was either stop and go back in the building, or try and jump this thing. Well, I tried to jump it, and I almost made it, but my one heel got caught and I hit the cement. And of course, this guy's yelling at me, but I just kept going.

My shoe almost came off, but half of my foot landed in the cement and I kept going. When I got back to the city room, Louie Clifford was sitting at the city desk, as he would sometimes, with his feet up on the desk, and he was spun around in his swivel chair, looking back behind him toward the hallway I came down, and he's waiting for me.

He spotted me, holding his finger up in the air, calls me there, and he holds up the phone and he says, "This is Judge Spellacy. She wants to speak to you."

The judge advised me that I was being held in contempt— we're going to take the word of your city editor, you're going to tear up that film, open it up there and tear it up in front of the city editor, three witnesses there. Which I did.

And all Clifford said to me was "You know what you did."

I said, "Yes."

"Do you understand?"

I said, "Yes."

He didn't say anything. He didn't chew me out or anything.

But then when Tanner came back, about 4 in the afternoon, and he read the riot act to Tanner.

BILL WYNNE
PHOTOGRAPHER, *Plain Dealer*

This day Sam Sheppard is heading for the Ohio Pen in Columbus. The cops are being very protective of him from the media. I am standing in a narrow corridor at the courthouse on East 21st Street. Sam is coming toward me with another prisoner cuffed to him on one side and a deputy on the other. Sam was always looking for sympathy from the public and he had a photo of his five-year-old son, Chip. He held it in front of him. After a quick shot I tore back outside to get near the unmarked sheriff's car in the back. A *Press* reporter locked the car doors with the keys in the ignition. The small group hustled to the car and the doors were locked. The cussin' was beautiful as one of the deputies had to go and get another set of keys. The photogs had a circus with Sam standing at the side of the car for 10 minutes waiting for fresh keys to arrive.

FRANK ALEKSANDROWICZ
*Photographer,* Press

I went to the Supreme Court of Ohio. I had never been inside. Nobody knew me. Everybody knew Sam Giaimo, the reporter. They said, "Hey Sam, whatcha doing here?"

The assignment was to take pictures in the Supreme Court. There's a little stand for the prosecutor to address the court. I was in the first row. I had an attaché case, a little leather thing. I practiced shooting with the camera indoors at home. Where there's a will, there's a way. It was silent. I had it taped up so you wouldn't see any glare. There were three big lamps at the end of the bench. I'm clicking away. I took about six or seven. I had to wind it by hand, but something wasn't right. I went out of that room with my attaché case to the bathroom. I got the camera out and checked it.

The film was not engaged. You have to be careful with a Leica. I went to the toilet, fixed it up. Thank God there was a young woman coming into the courtroom with kids. I waltzed in with the kids, sat down and continued my business.

I had my changing bag and I had my tank, chemicals, all ready and we went to the hotel room. I went in there and I loaded the tank with the film first, and I poured the developer, then after a given time, I poured it out. I pulled the film out. I was in the shower room and I had the light out.

I said, "Hey Sam, we got it." He said, "Call Louie." And we had that in the paper after a lot of discussions, double-checking so we wouldn't all go to prison. There was no byline for anybody. We handled this as a typical day in the life of a court. And that's how it came out. I should've milked it for another day or two. That was in 1958.

TONY TOMSIC
*Photographer,* Press

There was some house with people who died by asphyxiation, and we couldn't get the pictures—there were two young kids—but I saw the pictures looking through the window. I saw the pictures on the table there, and I just went inside the house and took them, and went back out the window. The house was wide open. The police lines there—things were very loose. Things were a lot different then.

BILL WYNNE
*Photographer,* Plain Dealer

At Ohio Penitentiary, I met Warden Cardwell and the assistant warden, who would escort me around to the key historic places and explain their significance. It was being closed down and replaced with a new facility at Lucasville. Sydney Porter was probably the most famous inmate. He's better known by his pen name, O. Henry. He began writing his masterpieces at the Pen.

The baseball field was later named in his honor, so the batter's box was a shot I had to get. There was a shot of one prisoner in a white T-shirt, his back to the camera working out with weights. Had to get that, as not many inmates were around. Next I snapped that simple little old brick building off by itself which looked innocent enough, but it was the death house. The death house and electric chair had dispatched about 325 men and women. Many of their pictures were there—somber faces and high collars or frilled dresses of the late 1800s and on into the 20th century. There were about 28 women among them and many of those looked as innocent as my grandmother. I took several shots of the photos on the walls. My host said one inmate who was skilled at electricity had rebuilt the chair to its present working order. He was convicted of murder. He met his fate in this chair he so meticulously reconstructed. The electric chair looked much like an old-fashioned office chair, but it had straps for legs and armrests. Then there were those electrical connections and dangling wires. At one point, my host asked me if I'd like to sit in the chair and have him take a picture of me. I was changing film at the time, but I said no. Another striking photo was the guard houses along the top the walls. In front of us, a guard with a tommy gun raised in the air watched us. The next day I developed my two rolls of film. The first roll was completely blank and the second roll was all double exposures. I figured out how I did it. I was a little shaky when I was asked to sit in the electric chair and instead of replacing the exposed film, I used it again.

Dudley Brumbach was the chief photographer and he looked over the negatives, using a magnifying glass. He thought some of them could be saved. It was unbelievable—two images, one on the inside of the cell and the other on the outside. We captioned it "Inside Outside." The shot of the electric chair made it look as if it were smack in the middle of the batter's box at O. Henry Field, and we captioned that one "Most Famous." The shot of the inmate in the white T-shirt was superimposed on the death house, and he looked like a ghostly figure, no head and no arms. So we captioned that one "Death House Ghost." The last ones we used were of Warden Cardwell and the outside guard. Cardwell was at his desk and the guard, with the tommy gun, was over his shoulder. We called that one "Forces." Yes, I believe in ghosts.

PAUL TEPLEY

*Sports Photographer,* Press

One of the things that might've helped me to get a job at the *Press* was an experience that I had with Frank Lausche. Frank, of course, was a senator and a Democrat who was known for voting against Republicans more than he was known for voting for Democrats. He was voting in an election at a school over on 40th and Payne and his wife Jane was with him, and we were in the basement of this place where the booths were. And they were talking and he started in to vote, and I just had an idea of what was going to happen. I thought, "He's going to go into the Republican booth." And sure enough he did. And as he hit the booth, his wife grabbed his arm, and that's when I shot the picture of him with a stunned look on his face and "Republican" over the booth. The *Press*, of course, loved the picture.

TONY TOMSIC

*Photographer,* Press

I was out on an assignment with Bill Tanner and it was raining. We heard that University Circle was under water. It was in the afternoon and the city desk didn't have anybody to send out and nobody believed the under water thing. We go to University Circle. We heard it really was under water, so I circled around and came from Shaker Square and went downhill to the top of that bridge and I saw an army duck coming down the street the same way are. Do you know what an army duck is? That's a boat truck with wheels, for dry land and in the water. And I looked down and I saw the water, and I thought, University Circle's a big lake. I handed Tanner the keys to the car and said, "I'm going on the duck."

Tanner thought I was crazy. I got on the duck and went for a boat ride on University Circle. We rescued an old lady out of her apartment, because that's what they were looking for. You know there's that apartment when you come down the hill? East Boulevard goes that way. And I got a lot of pictures that way.

That was the year the *Press* moved. I went to work that day in the old *Press* building and came back to the new *Press* building, literally.

FRANK ALEKSANDROWICZ
*Photographer,* Press

Tomsic went on an assignment which I refused to Louie Clifford, and I lived to tell you about it. The assignment was to cover Bruce Klunder, a minister who was going to protest. He lay down in front of the bulldozer and was run over and killed. I photographed his wife for *National Enquirer* one time later on. It paid $150.

TONY TOMSIC
*Photographer,* Press

When I worked at *Sports Illustrated*—the first thing people say to you in public when you work with *Sports Illustrated* is, "Have you done the swimsuit issue?" And my reply is that I'm not smart enough to do the setup pictures. If I have to think when I take a picture, I'm in trouble.

MARGE ALGE
*Society Writer,* Press

Frank Reed was very meticulous and an excellent photographer and the women loved him. Anyway, I'd egg him on to take as many pictures as possible. He would go back to the darkroom after a party, and when the negatives were ready, he would call me and I would go through the negatives with him to see which ones we should print, and not any other photographer would let you do that. We would have a few fights together and he would tell me what's wrong with the one that I liked, but I generally got my way.

# 11.

# "I had to wake up the widows."

[ LIFE ON THE DEATH BEAT ]

*Death is an integral part of life, and few stories are as reportable or readable.*

*Shondor Birns went up in a mighty roar, followed by flames and smoke. His appendages were scattered hither and yon. Superintendent of Cleveland Schools Frederick Holliday held the business end of a .357 Magnum over his heart and pulled the trigger. Retired* Plain Dealer *editor Phil Porter and his wife were murdered in their home.*

*Other stories about the recently deceased might be fascinating, for other reasons. At death, many lives, newspapers believe, become worthy of stories. For many readers, it's the best part of the paper.*

*Writing obituaries isn't easy, because the subject isn't talking. Others are, of course, and the first rule of obit writing might be accuracy.* The New York Times *is hardly immune from mistakes. In a death story about Walter Cronkite, the* Times *made seven (count 'em!) factual errors. There is no better way to annoy the survivors, and the disaster (and it was a disaster) will be part of every journalism course.*

*One of the unsung benefits of writing obits is the opportunity to meet such interesting people, even though the subject is no longer with us.*

**DICK FEAGLER**

*Reporter, Columnist,* Press

Sometimes I was the guy who had to wake up the widows. If there was a traffic accident or something overnight, you had to go down there and pound on the door and wake up the wife, who's been probably asleep for 20 minutes. Then you had to go in the house and get all the pictures of the dead guy. And I got pretty good at that. We'd take them all because the *Plain Dealer* was coming. Our cover story was "I don't know if I could tell how well any of these will come out. But our professional photo studio will know. With all due respect. I don't mean to cause you any further pain. This is the last picture of your husband that will ever run anywhere." And "I assure you you'll get them back." They did.

**BARBARA WEISS**

*Reporter,* Press

A cabbie went missing. His wife had called in and said that he never came home from work. The cops were out looking for him and investigating. I called the wife and she told me how he had called her, as usual, at midnight, 1 o'clock. She said that he always said, "I love you and I'll see you in the morning" before he hung up. And she just couldn't imagine where he was. He had been killed and stuffed in the trunk of his cab. So I was told to call her back and get information and the picture and everything. So I called back, and this was really hard to do because I realized that she did not yet know her husband was dead. So I had to make up a story about needing a picture in case somebody saw him. It was a hard, hard thing to do.

**TOM SKOCH**

*General Assignment Reporter,* Press

At the *Press* everybody did obits. There was a principal obit writer, but if she was busy, anybody else could get into obits if they were open. No big shot was too big a big shot to do some-body's obit. Everybody's got a story, and this may be their one shot in life to get into the paper so let's tell the world who they were and what they did. So we always tried to write the obits with some little hint of what this person's life was like.

One day I had the weirdest obit ever, I think, and they actually put a byline on it, which was unusual. This guy, I think, was a locomotive engineer by trade, but his hobby was to rent himself out as a heckler. He'd be like a vicious Don Rickles kind of heckler. He was a guy that would be hired to get up at a wedding and when they say, "Does anybody object to this," he'd get up and say, "She's carrying my baby," or something like that. He'd go into bars and accuse people of things. And they wanted that in his obit. That was what he did. I don't know what happened to that obit. I've got it someplace, I hope.

ALANA BARANICK
*Obituaries,* Plain Dealer

When I was working at the [Elyria] *Chronicle-Telegram,* I realized we needed to do more reporting on obits when Mrs. Moen died. She died in Florida. Florida funeral homes are notorious for giving you hardly any information. They faxed us something that said, "Mrs. Moen, who used to live in Elyria, is dead. And she belonged to the church in Elyria." And that was pretty much it. And that was pretty much how I wrote it up.

The obit went through the city desk people—no comment. It went through the copy desk people—nothing. Then it got to Joe Gluvna, who was the city editor. He chewed me out. He said, "Don't you know Mrs. Moen?"

"No." I really had no clue.

"Did you hear of the Moen faucet?" he asked.

"Sort of." But I didn't know what it was.

"Don't you know that the major employer in Elyria is Stanadyne, which makes Moen faucets?" he barked. "From now on, anytime you do an obit, you go back in the library and you look for stuff. Find out everything."

That wasn't being done regularly by anybody working on obits. Most of the people who knew to do that ended up getting better jobs.

LOU MIO
*Reporter,* Plain Dealer

There was a guy who used to hang around the *Plain Dealer* and at the Headliner and the other bars around the *PD*. Everybody called him GI Joe because he always had a field jacket on and maybe an army cap of some kind. Nobody really knew his real name.

One day, one of the guys came up to me in the office and said, "Did you see the little story in Sunday's *Plain Dealer*? It's two paragraphs about the guy that was killed by a hit-skip driver right down the street from the *Plain Dealer*."

"Yeah, I saw that," I said.

"That was GI Joe," he said.

"Oh, shit. He deserves more than three paragraphs."

I started to follow it up, and followed it up and followed it up, and peeled away a layer of his life at a time. When I was all done, I had a 50-inch obituary.

He always said that he served in the 82nd Airborne Division, and he was a fighter and he boxed and he did this and he was in a concentration camp. Well, it was all bullshit, but it was harmless bullshit.

It turned out, he wasn't a boxer. He lied about it. He wasn't in the Airborne, but he was in the Army. He was in Germany. He was a truck driver, I believe, for a medical unit. This was just after World War II. The funeral director had the death certificate, which had 82nd Airborne, so he didn't know the difference.

He got ahold of the 82nd Airborne Division Association. I'll be damned, if six of those guys didn't come out to the funeral and stand there. They didn't have a bugle, they didn't have taps, but they stood there at attention and gave him a salute, and damned if one of those Airborne guys didn't slap a decal on the urn.

When the story ran, it started on Page 1 and jumped twice. And never have I had more reaction that I did with that guy. This was before voice mail or before e-mail, and there were just stacks of those little pink notepads, so-and-so called, so-and-so called—I got calls from people who said, "Jesus Christ, I can't believe it. I knew that guy. I saw that guy all the time. I didn't know he had this background."

I never had more reaction to a story than with this guy and nobody knew who he was.

ALANA BARANICK
*Obituaries,* Plain Dealer

One day I got this information on George Ostro. He was in his late 40s and he was more or less an indigent person who had died in Rochester, which was a little tiny, itty-bitty 200-population village maybe, outside of Wellington. The funeral director who'd taken care of George didn't know a whole lot about him. He had a couple of sisters that the funeral director talked to. They weren't even sure where he was born. This is the kind of family we're talking about. And I said something to the funeral director, "Oh, I'll look in the files and see if we've ever written about George." He said, "Oh, you won't find anything on ole' George." So I go to the files, and lo and behold, there's George. George ran for president of the United States three times. He took out the petitions. He never got enough people to sign up to get him on the ballot, but he was interviewed because it was such a cool thing. And he was really crazy. That's really peculiar stuff. It was my first notion that you could write a really cool story about somebody who wasn't necessarily the former mayor or whatever. It was George Ostro, freethinker. It was cool.

DON BEAN
*Reporter,* Plain Dealer

During the early days of Vietnam, one of our duties was to call the families of the servicemen killed in Vietnam and get their story and get their history and get a picture. And I followed decorum. I followed tradition and asked the usual questions, no leading questions, and then finally, the job got to be so overwhelming, and the evidence that it wasn't a popular war—I finally departed from objectivity and started asking questions like "Was it really necessary for him to go to Vietnam?" "Was it really necessary for him to serve?" Maybe not quite that blunt, but pretty close to it. And never did I get an answer that it was unnecessary or that he died in vain. And I felt so many did. The families never said that they died in vain. It was a little surprising. I thought I'd find somebody.

BARBARA WEISS
*Reporter,* Press

I was put on obits at one point. That was a go-nowhere job. But I'll never forget Bill Tanner's line when he also wanted me to do engagements. I was hysterical and just, really, on the verge of tears. He said, "Well, why are you upset? This way, you get to marry 'em and bury 'em."

ALANA BARANICK
*Obituaries,* Plain Dealer

I got a call a long time ago at the *Plain Dealer* from a man in Florida who told me his ex-wife died. I'm asking him the regular questions, because at that point we were doing obits on just about everybody. We talked for a little bit, and then I asked him one of my favorite questions: "What set her apart from the rest of the crowd?" I like to ask people that. Some people are just so shocked, you can tell they have no idea what they're talking about. Others will tell you things that are wonderful. More often than not, you get, "Oh, he was a giving, caring person," that stuff. But this guy said, "She was 115 pounds when we got married, and she was 115 pounds when she died." I thought, no wonder you're not married anymore.

DON BEAN
*Reporter,* Plain Dealer

When things got slow on the police beat, that's when I got in trouble with my practical jokes and my practical stories. My made-up stories were not that frequent, but they were very, very successful. Bob Holmes was from England. And he was a very good reporter and a very good writer. And he came over here and he did very well at the police beat. He was going to law school. So one night, he was on obits for the first time. Now when somebody's on obits for the first time, we try to get a story to fake them out.

I was working a rare Saturday night. So I called the first time toward the first-edition deadline and I said, "This is the Donald B. Johnson Funeral Home in Northfield."

"Can't talk to you now," Bob said. "Can't talk to you now. Too busy. Too busy." And he hung up on me.

So at 10:30 I called back. Well, that was the deadline on Saturday night. I usually worked Monday through Friday and I was right on deadline, and I called Bob Holmes back, and this had to be the mid-'70s, '74 or so, and I said, "This is the Donald B. Johnson Funeral Home. I tried to talk to you earlier on, but you were too busy to talk to me. We have the body of Cyrus Eaton in here."

He said, "Oh!" And he started screaming. He said, "Vern." Vern Havener was on the city desk. He yelled, "Vern, oh, Vern."

And I started screaming, "Wait, wait!" And we got discon-

nected somehow. We didn't have any cell phones or hotlines in
those days. So I tried to call back desperately, but they were tearing out the front page, they were making it over, they were calling
Potsdam and Nova Scotia—Cyrus Eaton's peace tank, where he
tried to make peace with Russia before we did, long before we
did. He was a peacemaker and he was also a profiteer. Of course,
he wanted profits from Russia.

But in any event, they were calling the Donald B. Johnson Funeral Home. They were calling Cyrus Eaton's farm in Northfield,
where I used to work in 1946 in his flower garden for 35 cents an
hour. But anyway, I couldn't get a line back in. Finally, I had to
call a reporter in the city room and say, "Stop that Cyrus Eaton
obit."

"Yeah? How can I do that?" he said.

"You tell them Don Bean said to stop that, that I just made it
up," I said.

He was happy as hell that I was in trouble. We didn't get along
too well. And I waited for the phone to ring. It was Vern Havener.
He had the coldest, iciest voice I ever heard in my life. He said,
"What do you know about a Cyrus Eaton obit?"

"I know everything about it," I said. "I was trying to pull Bob
Holmes' leg."

"You'll be pulling your leg on the street," he said, and he hung
up on me.

I thought I was fired. I was down at Central Police Station at
21st and Payne Avenue. I was married at the time and had three
children. I had to walk up to the city room to show at least that
I was sober. I had to stand in front of Vern Havener—he was the
assistant city editor that night, for that day—with my hat in my
hand apologizing, and I didn't even wear a hat. Vern was a pipe
smoker, and there were thick clouds of smoke coming up from
this pipe, he was so angry.

And I had to separate the smoke to look him in the eye and say,

"Vern, Vern, this is the history of practical jokes in the newspaper business. I'm just trying to follow tradition and have a little fun." And the next voice I heard was from—and he's dead now—was from the staff drunk. He was the pet editor. He was saying, in a squeaky voice, "If the s.o.b. ever did that to me, I'd fire his ass."

To his everlasting credit, Vern didn't fire me. He didn't even tell the city editor about it. It circulated all through the city room, of course, but he never directly told the city editor. Years later, about six years later, 1980, I'm assistant city editor, day assignment editor—I was quite a drinker in those days—I came in to work with one of the granddaddy hangovers. The phone rang and it was about 10 A.M. and the voice on the other end said, "Don, what time this morning did Cyrus Eaton die?" I said, "Oh God, Vern. Don't do this to me?" He said, "Why not? You did it to me." And he hung up.

LOU MIO
*Reporter,* Plain Dealer

I did a story about a guy named John Doe. My wife had worked for the State of Ohio at the time they were moving nursing home patients around. She told me one of the patients was named John Doe. "This is what the State of Ohio calls him because they lost all of his records," she said.

I had to do a story on him. Nobody knew who he was. He didn't have much, just a few possessions, so I asked him if he needed anything. He said, "Yeah, I like music. It would be nice if I had a little radio. I'd like to listen to music during the day when there's nothing going on."

I quoted that in the article, which appeared on Page 1. The next morning, Bill Miller, who used to be a reporter for the *Plain Dealer*, said, "You know, that guy you wrote about? Before the day's over, he's going to open up a Radio Shack."

Well, a construction worker dropped off the first radio about

6:30 in the morning, and they just kept coming all day. And not only did he get a radio, everybody in that nursing home got a radio.

I don't know how long it was after that, maybe a year later, I got a call from the lady at the nursing home, and she told me John died.

"There's nobody to be a pallbearer," she said. "Would you be a pallbearer for him?"

And carrying that guy into a funeral home—he had nothing— I broke up. The funeral, I think, was at a potter's field someplace in Hamden Township or Thompson Township, and that's where he was buried. And on the stone was the name John Doe. That guy had nobody. He had nothing. He didn't even have his own name, but we gave him 15 minutes of fame on the front page of the *Plain Dealer*. We got him a radio. That was a tough one, carrying that poor old guy into the funeral home.

# 12.

# The Women's Department

[ WOMEN REPORTERS ]

*Don't kid yourself—women reporters generally held their own with men, though they didn't drink, smoke, belch or carouse as much.*

*Women who joined newspaper staffs were victims of the usual sexism; they succeeded despite the stupidity of chauvinism. They were valuable contributors to lots of departments: entertainment, medical, travel, theater criticism, society, police beat, columnists, suburbs and photography. They were less welcome at senior editor positions, labor, politics and sports, where men held sway.*

*Of course, women ran the women's department, and from there lots of good reporting and writing was created.*

*By and large, they were drawn to newspapers for the same reasons men joined up: It was the greatest job in the world.*

DORIS O'DONNELL
*Reporter,* News

At Rhodes High School, I got awards for being the fastest typist and I could take shorthand and all that because my mother said, "You're never going to be a newspaper reporter. You have to be a secretary like your cousins." She didn't think newspapers would hire women.

MARGE ALGE
*Society Writer,* Press

I was made the society editor, which was a big, big deal in those days. It was announced on Page 1.

In those days, we wrote basically from the Blue Book, which lists all the society folks in town. You just had to get on the phone and call them. It wasn't easy in the beginning until you got to know them. I definitely wanted that job. I thought it was a great job. It was a job where you worked very hard, but it had a lot of perks, too. You got to see stuff. I thought it was the best job in the paper because it was exciting and creative. You got to know that maybe so-and-so was going to be divorced, but you never could use it in those days because Louie didn't allow it. So you knew a lot of stuff that you couldn't print.

In the beginning we went after only the blue bloods, then in the mid-'60s things changed as the city changed. Actually, what we did was cover all the movers and shakers at this time during those two decades. Things were classy, sassy, and stylish. Everyone seemed young and beautiful and raring to go. I had a daily column plus a big theme picture page on Saturdays. That was whatever I chose.

Louie Seltzer loved society coverage, so you would get an idea of what you wanted to do—it might be pictures of something coming up in the future, it might be a theme thing on dogs or cats, or gardens, or swimming, diving, anything. Then you had to get them to do it and set them up. But you'd present the idea to the women's page editor, who would approve it, and if you thought it was questionable, maybe you had to take it to Louie, but Louie loved society. He loved seeing big stuff and he loved beating the other papers, and we usually did, in my judgment, although it was pretty hard working against Mary Strassmeyer. Mary was good, and it was fun. Mary was much more aggressive. First of all, she was with the *Plain Dealer,* and that had more of a class ring than the *Press*, and it was out first. So she had that advantage.

HELEN MOISE
*Food Writer,* Press

Marge Alge was hysterical. I remember when I first got there she asked me if I would help her cover the opera. I thought, "Oh, that would be exciting." So I said, "What do I have to do?" She said, "Find out what they have on, what kind of clothes they have on, who the designer is." I went up to this one man and I asked his wife, "Who did your dress?" And I wrote it all down and I'd take all these quotes. And he said, "I suppose you'd like to know what kind of underwear I'm wearing." I thought, "I'm going to use that." We came back and typed it all up and I gave it to her, and that's when she pulled out a bottle of Scotch, and the two of us drank Scotch until we went home, which was around 5 in the morning.

TEDDI GIBSON-BIANCHI
*Entertainment Critic, Medical Reporter,* Press

My real name is Theodora. I hated it for a while. I was named after my father. And believe me, it was a really tough go using that name or Teddi because I would get registered for, like, "Boys woodworking, boys gym," in junior high.

Journalism, for me, just sort of evolved. I started in high school, at John Marshall, working on the school paper. I really started because my mother encouraged me. I think she was trying to get me over my shyness.

HELEN MOISE
*Food Writer,* Press

One year after about the 200th call on how to stuff a turkey around Thanksgiving, a friend of mine called—Connie Cutlip, from Higbee's in the advertising department. Well, at least I thought it was Connie. She said, "How do you stuff a turkey?"

I said, "Okay, Connie, I've had one call after another here. I really don't have time to fuss around with that." So I said, "Shove it up your ass."

"I beg your pardon," the woman said.

"Come on, Connie. I don't have time. I don't have time to fuss around right now."

And she said, "Well, this is not Connie. What is your boss's name?"

At that time it was Barbara Bratel, and I thought I was going to get fired. So I hung up. The phone rings and I'm sitting there shuddering. Barbara picks up the phone and says, "Barbara Bratel, may I help you?"

The woman said, "Yeah, your assistant—I asked her a simple question on how to stuff a turkey and she said to shove it up my ass."

Barbara started to laugh and she couldn't stop laughing. I didn't get fired. She didn't have words with me. She was just laughing too hard. When I told Connie, she just about died. So every year after that, at turkey time, she would call and I'd catch her.

RUSTY BROWN

*Women's Page Reporter,* Press

In 1971 I was assistant society editor. While newspapers to-day scarcely cover social events such as benefit parties, opera openings or debutante balls, society got big-time attention then. Much of that was due—at least on the *Cleveland Press*—to the formidable persuasion of Marge Alge, who felt "her people" and what they did was worthy of extensive reporting. She had not one but two assistants. We interviewed and photographed people at a couple events a week. Our stories often got top-of-the-page, eye-catching layouts thanks to the great photographs of Frank Reed.

And the parties were dazzlers—creative themes and decorations, unique settings—and splendid fun to attend. One of my favorites was the annual benefit for the Cleveland Institute of Music held at Higbee's. It was undoubtedly the city's largest cocktail party and raised thousands of dollars for faculty salaries. The year I covered the event, September 1971, there were 3,000 partygoers, 100 musicians, and three-score dancers filling 10 floors of the department store. It was a sort of "around the world on an escalator" theme. Store displays changed countries and continents from floor to floor—from Moroccan bazaar to Indian wedding tent with lots of pillows and brass, to Japanese dancers with parasols, and swirling, barefoot Israeli dancers. Presiding over this extravaganza were genial Higbee's board chairman Herb Strawbridge, veep Robert Broadbent and their wives.

HELEN MOISE
*Food Writer,* Press

The genius of the paper was Jim Frankel from the Friday magazine. He used to edit my restaurant reviews. Every time I handed him a review, he'd throw it in the wastebasket. I'd have to reach in the wastebasket and put it back on his desk, because he was always in a bad mood.

Once, I had to make a change because there were three brothers who owned this restaurant—they're out of business now—who called me and said, "I understand you're doing the restaurant reviews." They never knew who I was when I was in the restaurant, then I would call them on the phone to ask a couple of questions.

They called me back and they said, "There are three brothers that own this."

"Yeah, I know," I said. "I've got all three names."

"Which name do you have first?"

"Well, what difference does that make?"

"It makes a big difference! If you don't put such-and-such brother's name first, he's going to kill me! He'll do this and he'll do that."

I said, "Okay, okay."

So I went over to Jim Frankel, the editor of the weekend magazine, and I said, "Jim, just get on the terminal and just put this name first and put this name second and this name third." He was so mad, he came over and he went crazy. He went absolutely crazy! He just kept screaming and screaming at me. So I picked him up by the seat of his pants—because he was just this little guy—and collar, and I dragged him from the women's department across the city room and threw him in his chair.

He was shaking. "I'm going to sue you. I'm going to sue you."

"Go ahead," I said. "I don't have any money. What are you going to get? Nothing. And don't ever talk to me like that ever again."

Frank Hruby came over to my desk after this whole thing was over with, and he said, "I wanted to stand up on my desk and do a dance and cheer for you, having the nerve to do what you did today. I go home with apoplexy every night. My nerves are shot, I have a headache, and all these things, because he puts me through so much every time I hand him a review."

Well, later Frankel calls me on the phone and says, "I'm crazy about you. I love you. You're one of the people that I like the most, and here I treat you like dirt. Please forgive me."

Of course, I did.

MARGE ALGE

*Society Writer,* Press

The *Press* sent me everywhere pursuing the right names and faces, in exclusive destinations like Aspen and Vail—anywhere in Florida, the Bahamas. I went on a freighter and did something on George Steinbrenner's farm. We did people in Nassau and Bermuda and in Europe. I went to Europe on assignment.

I always wanted to go with the Cleveland Orchestra, and in those years, the *Press* would send someone to cover what was going on when the orchestra toured. They told me that I would go at one point, and each time they would send someone else. I thought I was going to go to Japan with them, but they pulled it and they sent Feagler instead. And I was furious. And I went in—this time Tom Boardman was the editor, I remember, and I went in and I just blew my stack. I even surprised myself. He said, "Don't worry. You can go anywhere you want, some other place." He said, "Where do you want to go?" I said, "I would like to do the Dublin Horse Show."

So I went to Ireland for two weeks and did a series—I thought they were great stories—on the rich people connected with Cleveland in Ireland, including the north of Ireland. And one in particular I remember was the afternoon after the big show, there was a party for the American equestrian team at the American embassy. It was held exactly at the time that Nixon resigned. So everybody at the party—it was at this lovely manor house with the sheep grazing on the lawn—was watching Nixon resign. It was great, absolutely great.

TEDDI GIBSON-BIANCHI
*Entertainment Critic, Medical Reporter,* Press

I can remember having these weekly staff meetings about whether women would be able to wear pantsuits to work in the winter, because we were all freezing, walking to the office on East Ninth Street.

HELEN MOISE
*Food Writer,* Press

When Marge Alge retired, they gave me her job, which I knew nothing about, and I thought, "Oh my God, to go in at 8 in the morning and go home at 5 the next morning, after covering something." I had to take a cab home because I was scared to drive at that hour. I don't know how she did it. I only did it for a year and then the *Press* folded. She was a pro. She was always a lady. And she was very competitive with Mary Strassmeyer. They were the best of friends. And they had a great deal of respect for one another. But people at that time favored the *Plain Dealer* because it was Tom Vail and he was one of the gang—so Margie had to work a lot harder to keep her good reputation, and she finally got to the point where they really loved her and gave her lots of stuff.

TEDDI GIBSON-BIANCHI
*Entertainment Critic, Medical Reporter,* Press

I didn't run into much sexism as a reporter, but when I became home magazine editor and assistant women's editor, there was a lot of stuff, you know, making up pages first thing in the morning, and reading type upside down and trying to do things on the wing to get things to fit. That's when they had linotype machines. And the printers were—well, there were a lot of cat-calls and whistles, and you had to be careful you weren't going to get pinched and that sort of stuff. It was really hard because you needed their cooperation to get things done, and yet you had to restrain yourself from wanting to slug somebody. There were people, some senior editors—they're dead now—who used to say some fairly, well, they were more than flirtatious remarks, to me.

Later, when I was the medical writer, Julian Krawcheck would say, "Doesn't that bother you?" So it was there. Today, you certainly would, at least, have a place to lodge grievances. How could I—I thought I was just trying to be nice to people, or to get along with people, and I thought, "Am I doing something wrong? Giving off the wrong message or something?"

HELEN MOISE

*Food Writer,* Press

I was always having to do some kid's homework. "My kid is taking this course in chemistry class and he wants to know if he puts one ice cube wrapped in foil, one ice cube wrapped in wax paper, and another one in regular newspaper, how long will it take each one to melt?"

I said, "You're kidding me."

She said, "No."

I said, "Well, I don't do homework. I do food calls, but I don't do homework."

She said, "Well, he's got to know—he'll flunk his test."

I said, "Do you actually think I sit around here and wrap ice cubes in foil and in plastic and in wax paper and newspaper, and sit here and watch them melt? And figure out how long it takes each one?" I said, "I don't do that."

She hung up on me.

HELEN MOISE

*Food Writer,* Press

I did make some mistakes. A lady called me up at my apartment on Saturday morning, like at 8, and said, "Are you Helen 'Moiz'—instead of 'Moizee'—the one in the paper?" I said, "Yes." She said, "Well I have something to tell you. I just blew up a batch of cookies. They exploded in the oven." I said, "You didn't see the correction in the paper? Are you talking about the ones that called for, instead of a teaspoon of baking powder, a cup of it?" Wouldn't you have thought—nobody even has a cup of baking powder? It was a typo. We had it corrected in the next edition. She got the first edition. It was corrected in the next edition, because they always had to correct their typos. I'd go in the back room and had to read that type upside down, and to read something upside down, a quarter or a half, how can you tell? It was difficult because we used that lead, and I was always back there proofing everything upside down. So it was easy to make a mistake. So anyway, she was mad. That was probably one of the biggest mistakes I made. Another time the typesetter dropped a whole thing of metal lead that would go on the printing press— dropped it on the floor and it was a recipe that was in the paper and it got messed up because they just threw everything in after it had been proofed. And when the recipe came out in the paper, nothing made any sense, nothing. Absolutely nothing made any sense. Things like that happened.

HARRIET PETERS
*Television Reporter,* Press

There were times when things were difficult and I thought that I would quit, but that passed quickly. I would see people in other jobs in other fields, and I would think, "Oh, my gosh, that could have been me." I couldn't have possibly been as happy as I was at the *Press.*

HELEN MOISE
*Food Writer,* Press

In the late '60s, I believe, the women's movement started oc- curring. Things started to change in the late '60s because of the Vietnam War, more women were working, more women were in the workforce. Divorces were high at that point, not as high as they are now. At that time, one out of four people were getting divorced. Today's it's one out of two, but it was still high for then. So people had to go out and work. They had kids. Women had to go into the workforce, plus there was that war. I'm trying to think of the bra-burning days, which I totally ignored. I hated all of those women, because I never—you're not going to like this—I never wanted to be equal to a man because I always thought I was superior to a man.

# 13.

## "Too many martinis."

### [ DRINKING ]

*Bus Bergen was hardly the only Cleveland journalist to take a drink now and then. Newspapermen don't have the reputation for the drink that the Irish have. Still, they are hardly pikers when it comes to booze. Between the* Press *and* Plain Dealer, *different hours of operation meant a great deal:* Press *staffers generally worked 7 a.m. to 4 p.m. At the end of the day, with notable exceptions, most of them went home. The* Plain Dealer *started its day at 10 a.m. and finished during prime drinking hours. Hallowed haunts included the 2300 Club and Shai's, both on Payne Avenue, and the Headliner, just a block west from the* Plain Dealer *plant on Superior Avenue. The reporters mostly drank beer. Tom Kaib was one of the exceptions. He carried an eyedropper filled with vermouth in his pocket. He didn't trust any bartender to get the vermouth/gin ratio right.*

LOU MIO
*Reporter,* Plain Dealer

"Sleeve" was an institution at the *Plain Dealer*. I don't remember who started it. That was a sign when you wanted to go out in the middle of the afternoon for a drink—which occurred Monday through Friday. So you'd be sitting at your desk and, maybe 2 or 3 in the afternoon, somebody would be sitting on the other side of the room and just kind of tug at their shirtsleeve. And pretty soon, you'd look around and somebody else would be tugging his shirtsleeve. Well, it meant, let's walk out the door in our shirt-sleeves without our jackets to walk over to the Headliner to get a drink in the middle of the afternoon. So that just got shortened to "Where are you going?" "I'm on a sleeve."

Short sleeve, long sleeve, it didn't make any difference. But the point was, if you were out with your jacket on, they thought maybe you were going out on assignment or something. If you just went out in your shirt, they said, "Oh, well, maybe he's just down at the john or at the cafeteria." Well, we'd gone over to the Headliner, which was only a block away.

MIKE ROBERTS
*Reporter, Editor,* Plain Dealer

The drinking was unbelievable . . . the printers, the pressmen. Not so much the reporters—you couldn't be drunk and write, although there was a fair share of it among the reporters. I re-member one day, I came to work and there was a bulletin in the early edition of the *Press* that said our theater critic had a heart attack in the middle of Ninth Street. I said, "God, that's awful." A city editor looked at me and said, "He's back there working. He passed out in the goddamn street. He had too many martinis at lunch."

STUART ABBEY
*Reporter, Copy Editor, Editor,* Plain Dealer

My first date with Bobbie, who turned out to be my wife, was to a retirement party. It had management as well as staff. It was in the old Hollenden House Hotel and the state liquor depart-ment donated a case and there were other gratuities. The party dissolved into two groups, older staff and editors playing poker in one room and younger and poorer reporters drinking and BS-ing in the other. It started in the early evening and as deadlines came and went, more reporters and editors came in. Nice thing about *PD* parties, you could come early, start drinking, if you were of a mind, and stay all night.

JIM MARINO
*Criminal Courts Reporter,* Press

I still remember the night that I got word that I was being promoted from police beat to the suburban desk the next day. The *Plain Dealer* guys, as well as the *Press* guys, took me to a bar across the street from Central, where we got tremendously looped. I staggered back into the police station in time to have a *Plain Dealer* reporter introduce me to their new boss—somebody who had just been hired as a senior editor at the *Plain Dealer.* And as he stuck out his hand to me, I threw up on him.

BOB YONKERS
*Reporter, Editor, Assistant to Editor,* Press

Seltzer, maybe once a month at least, would gather a few of us. We'd all go to lunch at either the Union Club or the Mid-Day Club. Everybody would have a drink except Seltzer; he never, never drank.

BOB DANIELS
*Reporter, Rewrite,* Plain Dealer

The 2300 Club was a very, very interesting place. It was just a hangout for all types of people. It was owned and operated by a murderer, the late Nunzio Yapollo. He murdered a guy on Payne Avenue, as a matter of fact, maybe in the 1930s, and did time for it. I think he shot the guy to death, and the license for the bar, needless to say, was not in his name, it was in his wife's name.

He attracted all kinds of people in there—reporters, union people, blue-collar people. There were PR people and lawyers and students from CSU. It was just a real cross-section of people that went in there. We went there basically every night and closed it up. And all kinds of great things, and not so great things, happened in there. I mean, people used to get laid in the storage room in the back of the place. There were pinball tournaments. I saw a couple of dead bodies there—guys shot to death in the place.

One time, Tom Greer, Steve Hatch and I went over to the 2300 Club at lunchtime and we were drinking beer. And contiguous to it was a restaurant in the same building. There was a window between the restaurant and the bar. People in the bar could order food and they'd pass it through. And people on the other side could order drinks and they'd pass it through the other way. Now it was lunchtime and we got to playing pinball and drinking beer, and Hatch and Greer were both world-class belchers. I mean, they'd just belch raucously, almost at will, but especially when they were drinking beer. Well, they started belching and basically got into this belching contest—just one after another.

Finally, the barmaid said, "In the name of God, will you stop that belching?"

Well, they didn't. They just kept on. And finally, the guy in the restaurant got up and closed the doors to keep the belching noise out of the restaurant. But that was a hell of a place. There was a lot of lustful stuff that went on there. The 23 was just a real colorful place to be.

DON BEAN
*Reporter,* Plain Dealer

In 1959, there was one of the first hostage-situation bank robberies in the city anywhere in the U.S. And I was working for the *Cleveland News* at that time.

I had been out late that night and had been places where I shouldn't have been. I got in very late and very drunk. I came in to work and I'm sitting at my desk breathing softly, just trying to stay alive. So John Reese looked up and said, "Don, there's a police shooting out at 93rd and Lorain. Get a photographer and go on out there."

And I thought, "Oh, thank you God. I can go out and get some fresh air."

I went out there and the tear gas was as thick as you've seen at any time you've been in Vietnam or anything, but I got out of that car with Jerry Horton—one of the best photographers we ever had at the *News*, and we had some good ones. And he went to do his job and I went walking right down the middle of the street, and shots were going "Bang! Bang!" And I'm walking down the middle of the street and this tear gas is gagging me. And I was not only a good reporter, I was a very lucky reporter. A policeman had been first on the scene—in fact, later I had seen where the bullet had just creased his right pocket. I could still see that. And he looks up at me and he's crouched at the fender of a car and he says, "Get down, you damn fool. Do you want to get shot?" I said, "I'd be a lot better off."

LOU MIO
*Reporter,* Plain Dealer

I'm on an assignment with a photographer and he decides he would love to stop in the middle of the afternoon for about two or three quick drinks. We're on an assignment in Westlake or Bay Village dealing with little children who were HIV-positive. So I'm out there interviewing the lady who runs the home and we're waiting to see a couple of the kids because we want to get a picture of the kids.

One of the kids wakes up and the lady brings a little baby out, and they're playing with the baby and I'm sitting here talking to the lady. And I'm thinking, "How come there's no cameras going off? How come there are no flashes going off?"

So I turned around and there's the photographer on the end of the couch, head back, mouth wide open, sound asleep. The lady said, "He must've had a hard day." He didn't have a hard day. He probably had a hard night.

JIM RYAN
*Action Line Editor,* Press

I wrote a book review for Showtime Magazine and I was drunk, and I had this copy in my hand and I was trying to fix it. Anyhow, Louie Seltzer had his secretary call me in, and the business manager, and sat me down and said I was through. So I was fired. That was the end of the '70s. I ended up selling toilet seat covers in May's basement.

JIM MARINO
*Criminal Courts Reporter,* Press

One night I went to the Theatrical with a couple buddies from college. As we walk in, there's Bus Bergen face down on a table to the right of the bar as you walked in. With him are Jerry Milano, Jerry Gold and a female federal prosecutor. As I walked by, Jerry Gold grabs me by the arm and says, "Hey, your friend here is drunk. You gotta take care of him."

"You got him drunk," I said. "You take care of him."

"Hey, we gotta leave," they said. "If you don't take care of him, the bartender's going to call a paddy wagon and they're going to take him to the drunk tank.

Jerry Milano comes up and gives me 20 bucks and says, "Just go to the pay phone and call the Yellow Cab and have them take him home."

I knew Bus lived on Delaware Avenue in Lakewood. So I dutifully walked over to the telephone, called the Yellow Cab and they showed up. A couple of bouncers and I put Bus in the back of the cab. The cab driver says, "I'm not taking him anywhere. He's drunk. We've got a policy. If somebody's unconscious and drunk, we don't take him anywhere unless one of you sober people comes with me."

So I had to go with him. We drive off to Delaware Avenue. The taxicab driver and I drag Bus into the house. His wife is there with her eyes opened real wide at the sight. The next day I come in to work and I have to walk past Bus's desk to hang up my coat on the rack. And Bus, who always kept his head down but then looked up like the old professorial schoolmaster, says, "Hey kid." He called everybody "kid."

I walked over and said, "What?"

"I understand I got you to thank for last night."

"Hey, Bus, there's no need to thank me. You'd do it for me. Don't think anything of it."

"I wasn't going to thank you."

"What do you mean?"

"Well," he said, "you had no way of knowing this, but I walked out on my wife two weeks ago. I was living at the Hollenden House."

# 14.

# "Don't mess with the Guild."

## [ MANAGEMENT AND LABOR ]

*Somebody has to make sure the bills for ink and newsprint are paid; just after God invented newspapers, She invented management. Management's behavior often confused labor. Labor and management, especially in this town with its black and blue history of strikes, lockouts and picket lines (Local 1 of the Newspaper Guild was the first editorial union in the country), rarely shared the same vision, much less the same goal. The battles that were fought, the victories and the defeats, fade away and the lessons learned along with them.*

*When push came to shove at the bargaining table, labor's last weapon, a strike, was launched. According to an agreement between publishers, if one paper was struck, the other would lock out its employees. The agreement was closer to a mutual suicide pact than an example of brilliant management. Strikes rarely produce winners, but that doesn't mean the fight wasn't worth fighting. Management is driven by greed and labor is driven by the need to feed the kids and make the mortgage payment. Greed trumps.*

BRENT LARKIN
*Politics,* Press

My last day at the *Press* . . . Joe Cole buys the paper, and I'm not very smart, but I never had a good feeling about this thing. It just didn't smell right to me. And he calls me in one day. And I think Herb Kamm may have had something to do with this. But I go into Cole's office and he said, "How would you like to go fishing with Walter Mondale?"

I said, "I can't handle that. I hate to fish, Mr. Cole."

"Well, I know. If you want to go fishing with Walter Mondale," he persisted, "we can take care of that."

Well, the hell with that. I didn't want to go fishing with him, and I didn't have a good feeling about what he wanted to do at the paper even if it had succeeded. This was around the holidays of 1980. I put out a couple feelers to a third party. I never directly talked to David Hopcraft at the *Plain Dealer*, although I knew him pretty well. And so one thing led to another and I met in a secret room with Bob McGruder over lunch at the Cleveland Athletic Club.

They hadn't hired any *Press* people yet, except for one person, the year before that. That was Walt Bogdanich. He was my dear friend with the *Press* who came over to the *PD* as an investigative reporter. There were always rumors about you're not supposed to steal people away from each other because you don't want to start a bidding war for people's talents because they would cost the owners of the papers money. So my hopes weren't all that high.

As it turned out, McGruder said to take vacation for two months and quit the *Press*—"If you tell anybody where you're going to come to work, we may not honor our agreement." It might not have been two months, but it was at least six weeks. "You've got to take at least six weeks off and then you come in and we'll pretend like it's a new thing." And that's what happened. So I resigned and I had to lie to a lot of friends who kept asking, "Do you have a job?" But I wanted out of there. Obviously, in hindsight, I'm very happy with my decision. But Herb Kamm turned on me and attacked me after I showed up on the front page, after

I showed up at the *Plain Dealer*. It was very uncomfortable for me.

JIM MARINO
*Criminal Courts Reporter,* Press

This guy Herb Kamm comes in as the associate editor, and everybody thinks, oh, he's from New York, he's going to show us the New York way to do it. He's going to give us a shot of adrenaline. The *Press* is going to be great again. And the sawed-off son of a bitch was interested in absolutely nothing except promoting Herb Kamm when he came to town. He got his own television program, he got his own column, he'd fly to Israel and write a few stories, probably so he could write off the trip. The guy would go around and demand that reporters would step and fetch for him and give him their best items from their beats so he could use them in his "Herb Hears" column and act like he's the one that discovered the tip. He was a charlatan and creep of the first magnitude in my book.

BRENT LARKIN
*Politics,* Press

I liked Herb Kamm. He was very good to me, too. You had to take Herb for what he was, and he was a little bit self-absorbed. A lot of people thought he was into promoting Herb. Herb Kamm was a great gossip columnist. He had the Page One thing called, "Herb Hears." I contributed to it once in a while. Boy, he had sources. He came here from New York, but Herb was the ultimate schmoozer. He probably wasn't here two years and he had his own television show. Did he kiss too many asses in the corporate world and the political world? Yes, absolutely. And did he maybe, at times, try and protect a few too many people? Probably, yeah. And while he was a great promoter of Herb, he was also a great promoter of the *Press*. And I firmly believe that he loved the *Press*.

So I'm more willing to forgive some of those other things than others are.

TONY TOMSIC
*Photographer,* Press

Herb Kamm—I can't even remember the year he came. I got to know him. It was kind of weird. I got to know him because somebody told him I knew Art Modell. I don't know if they were fooling around or what. But I did know Art Modell, and he wanted to make contact with him because Modell was a New York guy. And Herb called me in the office and said, "I hear you know Art Modell, What do I have to do to meet him and talk to him?" So I reached in my pocket because I had a little book and I said, "Here, let's call him up." Somehow that impressed Kamm. I don't know why. But it did. And they met and had lunch and got to be friends.

STUART ABBEY
*Reporter, Copy Editor, Editor,* Plain Dealer

Remember the homicide in the Santa Claus line at Higbee's? Front-page story, but deep inside, down at the bottom, we identified the store. Big advertiser—we didn't put them up front.

JIM STRANG
*Reporter,* Plain Dealer

When Kent State happened, I was in a motorcycle shop out in Painesville when the shooting was going on. I had sort of a political awakening of my own at that point. I thought, "My God, they're killing us now." I was still close enough to Kent to consider myself part of the whole student body. I had been a fairly conservative Republican up until that point. Then I just became an anarchist. I let my hair grow. I had the hair and beard. Management wasn't big on having reporters with long hair. One day the managing editor sent a note out to the Lake County bureau and said, "When are you going to get a haircut?" And I wrote back on the bottom, "When are you going to transfer me downtown?" And it sure went downhill from there. I left the *Press* in September of '71.

ROBERT FINN

*Music Critic,* Plain Dealer

Management treated my beat—let's put it this way, most of them knew nothing whatsoever about classical music. They were interested, maybe, in other things. Maybe there was some interest in movies. Maybe they went to the Play House, or whatever, but I think they said to me when I was hired, "You know, I don't know very much about this kind of music." They trusted me—fools! But they did. But they were very supportive. They were sympathetic to me. You've probably heard from other people you've talked to about the snowflake. Do you know what a snowflake is? [A congratulatory note from an editor, typed on a half sheet of onion paper] I got my share of them and I have a file of them at home.

RUSS MUSARRA

*General Assignment Reporter,* Press

I remained a copy boy for three years. That was a reasonable time, in my case. I was only 18 years old. I started at the paper the day before my 18th birthday. They weren't going to promote me until I was legal. I got married April of '59, and about a month later, I got my promotion. I was still a copy boy. In fact, I remember that we were trying to buy a house. I was 21 when I got married. I was 22 years old and I was making something like $75 a week, and it wasn't enough money to qualify for the loan. I remember, I think it was Norman Shaw again, told me that I could tell the bank I was making more money and that they would back me up in the lie.

**GEORGE VUKMANOVICH**
*Copy Boy,* Press

If you started out like I did as a copy boy, and there was an opening on police beat, they'd put you on there if you wanted it. They changed that. Just as I was up for it, boom, they changed it. Scripps Howard didn't want it. They said they were going to get these kids from some newspaper from out in the middle of nowhere that have no idea what the hell the city's like or nothing else. That was it. I was stuck. I should've left then and there. But I kept thinking that they were going to change the policy. I was there 13 years altogether.

**JIM NAUGHTON**
*Reporter,* Plain Dealer

I once took offense when I got a note from Phil Porter, when I was on night rewrite, that said something like "Congratulations on your story on the boy who drowned in Lake Erie. It was written at the eighth-grade level." I huffed into Porter's office and said, "What do you mean by that?" He patiently explained that they had just begun using the Gunning Fog Index, named for two idiot professors, I suppose, and were determining the grade level at which *PD* readers could digest a story by measuring the length of syllables, words and sentences in a story. Ever since then I've taken perverse pride in things like an 87-word lead on a story I edited in Philadelphia.

**HARRIET PETERS**
*Television Reporter,* Press

An interesting point about Louis Seltzer in the early '60s: he prohibited the TV/radio department from doing interviews with local news people because he considered television was our big competition. It wasn't until I don't know how many years later that someone, not me, but someone convinced him that television is here to stay and that the audience really liked these people and considered them their friends, so it would be good for us to interview them because maybe they would read the stories, which is true. So then we started doing them frequently.

STEVE ESRATI

*Copy editor, Columnist,* Plain Dealer

Joe Eszterhas was canned after he described the *PD* as a "whore flying around the world with her legs spread." That sort of thing will generally lead to a firing.

[Eszterhas's 1971 article in the *Evergreen Review* criticized the *Plain Dealer* for making money off Ronald Haeberle's photographs of the My Lai massacre.]

STEVE HATCH

*Reporter,* Plain Dealer

I was never a Joe Eszterhas disparager. Some of my best friends were, and are, and that's fine with me. I found Joe to be an above-average hard worker who was always ready to go to the scene of the action. Some saw him as a big-story chaser and maybe he was. I guess that's how you get to be a star. As for his alleged problem with the facts, I never cared enough to investigate to satisfy myself one way or the other. Ironically (some would say) he got fired for telling the truth about the inner workings of "Ohio's Largest" and the media in general.

I believe that the Guild's taking his discharge to arbitration was—and remains—one of Local 1's proudest moments. And, as I discovered in my own arbitrations, Joe was not the real issue—it was the ability of media owners to suppress the truth, or at least one person's version of the truth. The battle had to be fought. Yes, the Guild lost, but that arbitration and several strikes in the '70s made a statement: "Don't mess with the Guild." Sadly, that attitude apparently has dissipated.

LOU MIO
*Reporter,* Plain Dealer

As a union leader, I thought Steve Hatch was outstanding. He was in there fighting for people all the time. He had a really deep conviction in what he was doing. He grew up in Altoona, Pennsylvania. I think he was a union member from the time he was a young man. He was the local president when I came downtown; Jack Weir was still the executive secretary, and Steve succeeded him. And I thought he did a hell of a job, very good. He was very forceful, a very firm believer in what he was fighting for. Some people didn't like him. They didn't like the way he looked. They said he looked like he dressed like Uncle Bill's mix-and-match.

BOB DANIELS
*Reporter, Rewrite,* Plain Dealer

Steve Hatch got a lot of stuff done that nobody else got done. And one of the biggest things he got done, although I didn't benefit from it, was he got the pension benefits increased at the *Plain Dealer*—to unbelievable levels. I mean, they were very, very poor. The benefits were very, very poor in years gone by. But Hatch got that job done. And it's probably unfair to say that he may not be as strong as others, because he was strong, and he was strong when the *Press* faced their crisis. There was danger of layoffs and massive loss of jobs over there when Joe Cole took over. And while it didn't work out the best financially for everybody, nobody lost their job. Hatch negotiated a deal where the wage rates stood still, but everybody was still working.

DICK PEERY
*Reporter,* Plain Dealer

Carl Kovac enjoyed drinking with union activists almost as much as he liked pursuing women, but he refused to join. Signing up was optional, but membership was permanent. One

Thursday, when everyone went to the Rockwell Inn to cash their checks, have dinner and get payday drunk, an attractive student copy aide sat next to Carl as if by accident. After a few drinks he asked for a date. She said she could not go out with someone who was not in the union. Carl said he would join immediately. On cue, Chuck Webster whipped out a card. Carl signed. He never saw the copy aide again, but he continued to pay dues as long as he was at the *Plain Dealer*.

MIKE ROBERTS
*Reporter, Editor,* Plain Dealer

Two weeks before I joined the paper, I went downtown to the corner of Euclid Avenue and Ontario Street, right there by the old May Company. There was a wonderful cop there, Joe Dober. He would direct traffic and take his coat off and act like a bullfighter with the buses. I just spent a week with him. I photographed him and I interviewed him. I talked to the people there. It was a good story, and on my first day of work I had a byline above the fold, along with three pictures. It was an incredibly exciting moment for me. But the photographers were all angry because I wasn't in the union and the pictures violated work rules.

TONY TOMSIC
*Photographer,* Press

Unlike a lot of publications today, the *Press* was very much behind me with my freelancing anything I did. If I got a cover on a magazine, that was a story. They wanted to know about it. But going along with that, it was kind of a two-way street. If I found out something, I would tell them. Like, for example, when Frank Robinson was named manager of the Indians, it was a very big story because he was the first African-American to manage a team. It was a big national story. I remember *Sports Illustrated* called me up and said to go to the press conference. They knew what was going to go on. I said, "I'm going to be working for the paper." They said, "Well, you can work it out." It was always like that. So I went to Louie Clifford, and I was always up front with him. And as a little inducement, I said, "What if I got you a picture," because it was for the final edition—I said, "What if I got you a picture, not just of Frank Robinson—what if I had his wife thrown in there?" Because the *Press* was very family oriented, the wife or kids were as important as the guy himself. The whole thinking process of newspapers was different then. The *Press* was like a family newspaper or something. They were very big on family. But I told Clifford that because I'm also going to be working for *Sports Illustrated*, I wouldn't be able to come back to the office to make the edition, so somebody would have to bring the film back. He said, "Go do whatever you want. If you get the picture of the wife, we don't care what you do." And I did. I got the picture of the wife and sent it back.

HARRIET PETERS
*Television Reporter,* Press

When people would tell me how fat Jim Frankel was I couldn't believe it, because by the time that I knew him he was tiny, a very tiny man. He exercised every day. He took a long lunch hour with permission from the editors to exercise and swim in the pool at a Y or at a hotel pool. He was just very dedicated to staying slim. He was a very quirky person but brilliant, difficult to work with but he was one of the best mentors that I ever could have had, in helping me with writing ideas and creative ideas. I owe a lot to him. One thing that stands out in my mind, it's kind of silly, but when he later became editor of the Showtime Friday magazine, and daylight saving time was ending in the fall, he thought it would be cute to run a picture of West German Chancellor Konrad Adenauer with only the headline "Daylight Saving Time Ends." It took me a while, I didn't get it. Do you get it?

DICK FEAGLER

*Reporter, Columnist,* Press

In 1965, Louie Clifford assigned me to go down to University Hospital and write a three-part series on CPR, on heart massage, because that was just coming in then, when they thought everybody ought to know how to do this. So I took the course and I did it and really didn't think any more about it. One Saturday— I worked Saturdays—Clifford was going to go on vacation, and for some reason, he swung by the office. He had his wife in the car with him and he swung by the office to get something, and he saw me. I was doing a rewrite because we had a jumper on some bridge. So I just happened to talk to Louie. And he left, and pretty soon you hear over the intercom system, "Anybody who knows CPR, please come down to the Ninth Street door." And of course, I start looking around hoping somebody else could do CPR better than I, but nobody materialized. So I went down there and it was Louie. He had gotten down to the corner in his car and rolled it down to a stop opposite the door on Ninth Street and was slumped over the wheel. So I tried to do what I could do. The first mistake was I was pushing on Louie, but Louie was on a seat, so I had dragged him out and put him on a hard surface. I wasn't getting anywhere with that. I yelled for an ambulance to come and an ambulance came. It was too late, I'm sure, by the time I got down there and got to him because he had had a couple of previous heart attacks. So I rode over in the ambulance to St. Vincent with him and his wife. I went into the room. She stayed out. And they took his watch off and handed it to me and that was the last I saw of Louie until the funeral. I gave the watch to his wife. But I thought that was pretty ironic that he assigned me to this series and I ended up trying to use it on him. Then I went home and got drunk and cried.

# 15.

# Top Dogs

### [ LOUIS SELTZER AND TOM VAIL ]

*There could have been two editors more different than Louie Seltzer and Tom Vail, but only if other universes were included in the search. Louie was short, bald, devoted to his newspaper and his troops, given to lighting firecrackers in the city room, and finding himself at the receiving end of horseplay (he was once locked in a stall in the men's room, another time stuffed into one of the big wastepaper baskets in the city room). His advanced education started and ended at the* Press. *He had enemies and virulent critics, with good reason. But Louie managed to inspire loyalty among the troops. He loved his newspaper and he wrote his own stuff.*

*Tom Vail was to the manor born: blue-blooded, Ivy League, handsome, and appointed by family to lead the newspaper. He was aloof and elegant. If he had a sense of humor, he kept it well disguised. When he retired, the story in the paper told of disgraced President Nixon's call to Vail. Vail was playing golf and told the messenger that before returning the call, he would finish his round. His best stuff was written by others.*

DICK FEAGLER
*Reporter, Columnist,* Press

Louie Seltzer was the editor of the *Press* at a very young age. He was 28. And he kept that job for a good amount of years. By the time I got to know him, he was pretty much on the creamed-chicken circuit. He occasionally sat down at the city desk and took phone calls. But Louie had a rather mischievous sense of humor. He was about 5 feet, 4 inches, I'm going to guess. He was pretty active. I was always pretty big. I wasn't quite as fat as I am now, but I was always big. And he would come up to the big guys in the office and punch them in the stomach as hard as he could just for the hell of it, or he'd light a string of firecrackers and throw them into the room.

He had a private john in his office but he never used it, he always went out and used the regular john that we had. And one time he was in the stall and somebody barricaded him in. He had to climb over the top of it.

There couldn't have been a better guy to work for than Louie Seltzer. He took care of his employees. I never knew an employee who went on sick leave where Louie told them, "You've got $x$ amount of days to get back to work," or something like that. Louie always said, "You stay home as long as you need to stay home until you're able to come back to work." That's the way things were done then. It was a great experience. I'm certainly glad I was a part of it.

BILL TANNER

*Reporter, City Editor,* Press

I was proud of the *Press*. At that time, the *Press* really was ahead of the *Plain Dealer* in circulation and everything. It was the people's paper, and Louie Seltzer was the best-known person in Cleveland. I was very proud of it, especially with Louie Seltzer, because it wasn't long after that that *Life* magazine called him "Mr. Cleveland," and *Time* magazine—it was 1953, '54—selected the best 10 papers in the country and the *Press* was one of them.

Louie loved to sit in the city room. He'd come out in the city room, which had a big bank of desks. He loved to sit at somebody's empty desk when they weren't there, to use the phone. His secretary would always send the calls out to him wherever he happened to sit. He often sat next to me. One time I hear him say, "I think you ought to marry that girl. I think you ought to marry her," in a high voice. He hangs up and I said, "What the hell was that?" He said, "That was Eddie Fisher asking me if I think he ought to marry Debbie Reynolds." I said, "Did you tell him yes?" He said, "Of course I told him yes." He was known everywhere. I know he used to get calls from Danny Kaye, and John F. Kennedy called him the day before he made his inaugural address. Kennedy was calling a number of editors around the country. Well, I could talk forever about Louie Seltzer.

HARRIET PETERS
*Television Reporter,* Press

The building at East Ninth and Lakeside opened in 1960, and that was the year I started there. Louis Seltzer was so proud of the building. Of course being new, it was spotless and he just couldn't stand to see any mess, and he, as you probably all know, had a reputation of being immaculately dressed with a satin handkerchief to match his tie, and he would go up and down the aisles, bending over, picking up all the scraps of paper.

DICK FEAGLER
*Reporter, Columnist,* Press

He was wildly independent because the *Press* was a Scripps Howard paper. Scripps Howard was a chain and we were part of that chain, but Seltzer was making so much money for the *Press* compared to the other Scripps Howard papers that the chain didn't really have that much enforcement ability to tell him what to do. And that was most famously indicated when in 1960 the chain endorsed Nixon for president and Seltzer ran it, and the

*Press* endorsed Kennedy. They ran both editorials side by side. Seltzer liked Kennedy. So he had a lot of power.

WALLY GUENTHER,
*Investigative, General Assignment Reporter,* Press

Louie Seltzer was a down-to-earth person. The guy never went through high school. I think he dropped out in the eighth grade and started from scratch in the business. He was feisty. His influence in the paper itself, with the young reporters—he could walk into the city room and you could just walk over to him and talk about a story you did. But he had a great influence on the city and he liked people. I think a lot of *Press* readers felt close to him because of some of the projects he had the *Press* do that involved, not only the news, but people getting involved in neighborhood situations.

BOB YONKERS
*Reporter, Editor, Assistant to Editor,* Press

I was service director at the time, right outside of Seltzer's office. Bob Hope would sit in the corner there and fill Seltzer with anecdotes and stories. Bob Hope bought Seltzer a golf cart to get around—I guess when his wife Marion died, Seltzer went to live with his daughter out in Spencer Lake, near Chippewa. It was a pretty big property, I remember, a lot of acreage. Hope shipped him a golf cart. Seltzer had a lot of favorites, in the department and in the city—Celebrezze and Locher

He made sure we gave them adequate coverage when they were running for office. Of course, they both did well. Frank Lausche was another buddy of Seltzer's.

There really wasn't a connection between Seltzer's office and city hall, though, not even when they moved to Ninth and Lakeside. Seltzer would come in at 5:30 in the morning. And I once said to him, "How can you come in so early every morning?" He said, "Yonkers, if these fellows come in that early to go to work for me and put out our newspaper, I want to be with them and give them my support." I said, "Louie, you don't have to do that for me."

He and I got along great. He didn't want to retire, you know. He fought that tooth and nail. Norman Shaw was the associate editor, and he kept nudging him. He said, "We're planning a retirement dinner for you. You've got to let them know that you're going to give in. You have to accept it." He said, "Goddamn it. I'm not going to. They'll have to carry me out of here."

DORIS O'DONNELL
*Reporter,* News

Daniel Rhodes Hanna was the most marvelous publisher. I just adored Dan—big, 6-foot-3, and always came out in the newsroom and talked to all the reporters. It was such a family affair in the newsroom. It was family. It truly was at the *News.* Everybody kind of stuck together because we were the underdog newspaper. We had to try so much harder against the *Press* because Louie Seltzer was such an egomaniac. He thought he was the kingmaker of Ohio and all that crap.

STUART ABBEY
*Reporter, Copy Editor, Editor,* Plain Dealer

Do you remember the governor in "The Best Little Whorehouse in Texas"? He was always disappearing—now you see him, now you don't. That was Tom Vail. The few times I saw him in the city room, he was always disappearing around a corner or behind a pillar in case one of the staff should want to talk to him. The little rich boy whose father got him a job and he couldn't cut it. Everybody else knew it, but he didn't. Tom Vail came of age and his family decided he should work in the business. Vail was given a reporter assignment. This guy should not be allowed near a typewriter. His columns were written by Bill Barnard.

GEORGE CONDON

*Columnist,* Plain Dealer

"I had an office about 30 feet away from Tom Vail for 22 years, and in 22 years he never once spoke to me, never said hi, or what the hell do you do here; we never had a conversation."

V. DAVID SARTIN

*Reporter,* Plain Dealer

I liked Vail a lot. I'm not sure why. We did not have a lot in common, him being blue blood. But I just got along with him real well. He was distant in the sense he was the publisher and I was the last man on the totem pole, but I liked him.

JIM NAUGHTON

*Reporter,* Plain Dealer

I think I owe some of my development at the *Plain Dealer* to the direct involvement of Tom Vail. One night I was on rewrite and he came out to the city desk and had a conversation with an editor (it might have been Russ Kane) and asked who could help him with a speech. The editor aimed him at me, and for some time afterward I wrote many of the speeches Vail gave around the city. I recall having to go to his office and have him tell me more or less what he wanted to say and then stitching it into a draft, triple spaced and all caps, that he would amend or approve. Some colleagues were offended that he didn't write his own stuff, but I wasn't, because I thought it was best for the paper and its own development if his speeches were coherent.

BOB DANIELS

*Reporter, Rewrite,* Plain Dealer

I didn't know Tom Vail very well. I met the guy a few times. I had drinks with him. In my opinion, he was basically a well-intentioned buffoon. He couldn't write his name. He didn't have a clue about life as it really is. People criticized him for that, and they criticized him for that accurately.

DICK PEERY
*Reporter,* Plain Dealer

A lot of the reporters did not appreciate Tom Vail because he seemed distant, but I thought it was great that he didn't get in the way. I did sense that he had journalism instincts. When he wrote an op-ed piece that I strongly disagreed with, I wrote one that I thought devastated his arguments. He was always warmer and friendlier after that. But he never invited me out to his Hunting Valley estate. I remember telling a mid-level editor that we would miss Vail when he retired. He said I was crazy. Later, the editor told me I was right.

# 16.

# "The hobnobbing was fantastic."

[ SUCH INTERESTING PEOPLE ]

*Reporters met presidents and royalty, ballplayers and movie stars. Ted Williams gave Bob Dolgan a batting lesson. Lorin Maazel gave Rusty Brown a kiss. But they all liked to see their names in the newspapers.*

BOB DOLGAN

*Sports Reporter, Columnist,* Plain Dealer

Ted Williams was the first guy I ever interviewed at the ballpark. He had a reputation of hating sportswriters. So I'm doing a sidebar and I go out on the field and I see him standing behind the batting cage by himself. I figured that if he yelled at me nobody else was around to hear it. In those days you could talk to people at the batting cage. Today they don't let you. They say they're working now. Everybody used to hang around the batting cage and talk to the ball players. You'd get a lot of notes that way. So I walked up to Williams and I said, "Ted, this is my first day on the job. I'm a writer with the *Plain Dealer.*" He looked at me and said, "How come they always send you new guys to me?" So I felt better right away. At least he wasn't yelling. He gave me a half-hour interview, which wound up with him drawing a plate on the ground and showing me how to hit the outside pitch.

**MARGE ALGE**

*Society,* Press

The hobnobbing was fantastic. You had a chance to brush with royalty. I drank a martini with Princess Margaret at a party. She was at the 20th Century Club. The 20th Century was a very social ladies' group that's still going, by the way, only now it's the 21st Century Club. She was one of the guests. I didn't see her that long, she was a little bit aloof, but she had a martini and I did, too. There were some other people within that. Prince Charles was here at one point, too.

**BURT GRAEFF**

*Sports Reporter,* Press

Nick Mileti impressed me because he was able to buy all these things with other people's money. The NBA, the Barons, owned the Arena, the Indians . . . Finally it all blew up. But he built the Richfield Coliseum . . . that was most impressive. He invested virtually nothing. He was a real promoter.

**JIM MARINO**

*Criminal Courts Reporter,* Press

Jerry Milano, probably the most colorful of the defense lawyers, used to drive a convertible Lincoln and used to drink at the Theatrical on Short Vincent. My first day in criminal court, he said, "Hey, are you the new *Press* reporter? Well, then, you've got to know me." And he was bragging about all his possessions, "You see this briefcase? This is Moroccan leather, kid." Then he'd throw me in his Lincoln and we'd drive down to the Theatrical.

One night at the Theatrical he said, "You can't tell me that these guys sitting here at this table are sophisticated organized crime leaders . . . He still hides his cash in tomato cans that he buries in his backyard . . . He's the one who refers to an affidavit as a 'happy David' because he still doesn't know English well."

I remember him getting razzed all the time about his wardrobe and he'd say, "Vegas, baby. I bought this stuff in Vegas. You just don't find this kind of stuff in Cleveland. You can't find patent-leather purple shoes in Cleveland."

I thought to myself, "Thank God."

MARGE ALGE

*Society,* Press

I covered all the inaugurals. I covered the inauguration of Johnson. I did his and did two Nixons and did Carter's. I know it sounds silly, but we would get the Clevelanders that were there—any Cleveland connection—and we would follow them to the balls that they went to, or whatever. Then we usually had coverage of that time, maybe, no more than two days.

All of our stuff had to be sent Western Union. I can remember taking taxis to Western Union at two and three in the morning almost every place we went. You didn't call it in. I can remember only one time I called my stuff in. It was for the America's Cup race up in Newport.

BOB DOLGAN

*Sports Reporter, Columnist,* Plain Dealer

I used to do a lot of stories on Howard Cosell. He was a funny guy, you know. The first time was when he was going on television, on Channel 5's "Morning Exchange" program, I went down there to do a piece on him. Off camera he went up to Liz Richards, one of the stars of the talk show. She was pregnant and he pats her belly. He said, "Take good care of our baby, Liz," and everybody laughed.

He started walking out and got in his limo and I introduced myself and said, "Howard, do you mind if I get in the limo with you? I'd like to talk to you." He said, "Yes, I do mind, but okay, you can come in here." So I sat down with him and we had a good interview. He told me to get out of the newspaper business. He said, "It's a lousy business, Bob. You're a good guy. Get out of it."

Another time I went to the hotel again to see him. I was talking to him for half an hour. He said, "I gotta get going now. I've got to go downtown for the game."

"Well, I'll drive you," I said. "Let's go in my car. You drive so I can take some notes."

"I'm sorry," he said. "I never learned how to drive."

HARRIET PETERS
*Television Reporter,* Press

Another person you wouldn't expect who actually caused people to stop working and stare was Tiny Tim. Again, I don't know if people remember him. He was in his heyday at the time that he came up to the *Press.* He was a frequent guest on the "Tonight Show" and actually had his wedding to Miss Vickie on the "Tonight Show". Tiny Tim with his full white makeup and lipstick and long curly hair. He was kind of ahead of his time if you think about it. He really caused people to stop work and come and just stare.

RUSTY BROWN
*Women's Page Reporter,* Press

Here's a moment I've never forgotten: Shortly after Lorin Maazel—so very handsome and continental—was named Cleveland Orchestra conductor in 1971, he and his pianist wife, Israela Margalit, were introduced to members of the orchestra women's committee. It was a Q and A event at Severance Hall, and I was assigned to cover it. Afterwards, I met him personally. As I was introduced, he raised my hand to kiss it, his eyes never leaving mine. I was so flustered, I dropped pen, notepad and purse. He helped me pick everything up.

MARGE ALGE

*Society Writer,* Press

We had to do all the ethnic debut parties—the Poles, the Hungarians, the Slavs, everything. I hated it. The only one that was done very well was the Polish one. The Polish did a very good one. They would have a lovely one. And the Hungarians were pretty good. I think among the debutantes themselves, the Hungarians were the best looking. The Hungarian girls were beautiful.

PAUL TEPLEY

*Sports Photographer,* Press

I got all kinds of assignments. I covered Miss America two years in a row in Atlantic City. That was somewhere around 1957 and '58, I think. That was terrible. Who'd like to hear Burt Parks sing "There she goes, Miss America" all week long? You're there for a week; it's not just for the competition. You're there all week. Back then, that was a big thing. Every newspaper in the country wanted to get pictures of their contestants. So you'd start at 8 in the morning and work until 2 the next morning, and go back and do it all over again for a week. It was not a lot of fun.

REED HINMAN

*Sports, Suburban Reporter,* Press

Bob August comes to me and he says, "The Indians have a road trip to New York and Detroit, and we need somebody to go. We'd like you to go." I'm pretty nervous about this. I'd been at the *Press* maybe six months. So I go on this road trip and we're staying at a hotel in Manhattan. The Indians had a fairly well-known pitcher at that time, Dean Chance. He'd been around, but he was fairly new to the Indians.

The *PD* baseball writer then was Russ Schneider, who was considerably older. I had just checked in and my phone rings, and it's Schneider, who I hardly know, saying, "Dean Chance and some of his friends want to go out on the town, and they wanted me to go, but I don't want to go, so why don't you go?"

Then Chance calls my room and he said, "Hey, it's not going to cost you a cent. It's me and one of my friends. It'll be fun." So I agreed, reluctantly, to go. Dean Chance and his friend from New Jersey, and me, plus three women. The guy from New Jersey is driving. We're driving around Manhattan. The first thing we do is we go to the Rainbow Room, in the RCA Building, for dinner. I guess the one girl was Chance's girlfriend, or something, and the other two were just, who knows who they were? I still had a crew cut from my military days.

It was exciting. I hadn't even been to New York. The next thing they want to do is they want to go to the Copacabana—in those days, it was a famous nightclub where Tom Jones was performing. The entrance to the Copa was jammed with a sea of people. Dean Chance, who was about 6 feet, 4 inches, gets fairly close, raises his hand to the doorman, and it was as if the sea parted. The six of us get ushered up to the front, taken to a table, and three minutes later, there's a bottle of scotch in the middle of the table.

I'm thinking, "Oh, boy, I'm in way over my head." I drink beer and an occasional glass of wine, but this is way over my head. So I'm trying to make small talk with this woman who was assigned to me for the night—heavily perfumed, heavily made up, probably 15 years older than me. I excused myself to go to the men's room. I go to the men's room and there's an attendant passing out hand towels, and there's this big jar with all these $5 and $10 bills in it. I'm thinking, "I've got to pay to go to the bathroom here." So I look in my wallet and I've got a couple of singles, so I threw a couple of singles in there. Tom Jones performed and the night broke up and I went back, and Schneider says, "Well, how was it?" I said, "Well, it was pretty interesting." But I still remember the thing about Dean Chance, how people just parted.

**MIKE ROBERTS**
*Reporter, Editor,* Plain Dealer

I was covering the White House. One day, Ron Ziegler, who was Nixon's press secretary, came out and there were only four of us in the pressroom. It was about 3 o'clock in the afternoon. He said, "You guys, the President wants to talk to you." I thought he was kidding. We walked right in, and Nixon's sitting there with his feet on the desk. He says, "Hi guys. How are you doing? I thought we'd talk a little bit about some of the questions that came up in the last press conference that we couldn't get into too much." We sat there for an hour and a half, came out, and had a good story. He was a smart guy. In a one-on-one situation, he was far more interesting and far more relaxed than he would appear in public.

# 17.

# This Job Could Kill You

[ HAZARDOUS ASSIGNMENTS ]

*Reporters rarely wore flak jackets. Neither were they always out of harm's way. Getting to stories, for both photographers and reporters, meant first finding the unmarked path to the action. And, man, was there ever action. Riots made parts of the city a free-fire zone and a minister, in a protest for civil rights, was crushed by a bulldozer. Bombs were the weapon of choice for gangsters, a suburban police station was blown up and on more than one occasion, hostages were taken.*

WALLY GUENTHER
*Investigative, General Assignment Reporter,* Press

Of course, you know I infiltrated the Klan. That was Louie Clifford's idea. In 1965, I think. Only Louie Clifford, me, and the photographer, Clayton Knipper, knew I was involved in this—nobody in the city room, nobody on the desk.

Clifford knew there was a Cleveland chapter of the Klan, so I wrote several irate letters and they finally asked me to come to a meeting. It was in Cleveland on 41st and Clark. I dressed in old clothes. My wife was a little edgy about this. She dropped me off, and as she pulled in the driveway to leave she saw a guy step out the doorway and follow me around the corner and down the street toward the hall where they were having their meeting. But she went on home. She had no idea who the guy was. Well, the guy turned out to be Sergeant John Ungvary, the head of the Cleveland subversives unit. And I knew him.

So he comes up to me and says, "Where are you going?" And I told him. He knew the meeting was going on. He and a couple of other police officers were hidden around doing surveillance.

"You can't get in," he said.

"I'll talk to you later on," I said.

He actually ran into a cemetery and hid behind a tombstone. But, anyway, I went to about eight meetings. Every Monday, John Ungvary would call me and ask me if I had any names. Well, it wasn't a place where everybody introduced himself. I'd go back to the *Press* and write notes. Knipper was taking photographs of the hall, discreetly. After my last meeting, I dropped out and went and wrote the story. They eventually broke up the Cleveland group.

After we published the story, I went back to some of these people and tried to talk to them. Then we had a series of threats. They were calling me at 3 in the morning, playing racial records, calling me at work saying, "You'll be walking up Ninth Street and get a bullet in your head."

I spoke at a community meeting one night out in Woodmere. The Klan showed up there and harassed me. The Cleveland Heights police put a 24-hour watch on my house. That put my wife really on edge. They were a threat. One night when I came home and pulled my car in, an unmarked car pulled in behind me and two guys got out. They were Cleveland Heights detectives. That's how close they were, watching the house. It took about a year before that settled down. As a young reporter, I loved it. I wouldn't do that now.

PAUL TEPLEY

*Sports Photographer,* Press

The miners' strike—a bunch of small mine owners were being struck by the coal miners. I guess they must've been United Mine

Workers. It was a very tense situation with a lot of hard feelings. I was told to go get a picture of some of these miners sitting on the steps of city hall. So I went down there. It was in Hazard, Ky., eastern Kentucky. So I went and tried to get what they wanted. And this was in the Speed Graphic days, which was 4x5 film. I also carried a roll of 2¼-inch camera film.

I walked up and decided I would try to approach this as nicely as I can. I walked up to a couple of miners sitting there and I talked a little bit. I said, "Would you mind if I took a picture of you guys sitting on the steps here?"

One of them said, "Which of those two cameras are you fixing to use?"

"I really don't know. Why do you ask?" I said.

"Well, I'll tell you. If were you, I'd use the small camera," he said.

"Why?" I asked.

"It won't hurt so much when I shove it up your ass."

That's my coal mine experience.

WILLIAM F. MILLER
*Reporter,* Plain Dealer

On January 17, 1967, at 1283 East 17th Street, I ran into a fire. I was walking out of the [*Plain Dealer*] building. It was cold as the devil and I had parked my car on Hamilton Avenue. As I came out the back door there was hardly anyone around. I noticed a roof was on fire. I knew that roof because that was where the poorest of the poor alcoholics lived. I just knew these men would not leave that building, so I came to the front door, knocked it out, and here the guys were sitting around drinking. The whole top floor was on fire, so I started screaming at them to get out. Some did, but some didn't, so I ended up grabbing and throwing them out the front door to get them the hell out of a burning building.

Well, there were 17 of them and I got all 17 out. So they were all huddled together, grumbling, and a fire truck is coming down the street. One of the fire chiefs came by and asked, "Did you get anybody out of upstairs?"

They were only on the first floor when I saw them. I said, "I got everybody out I found," and he said, "Let me go in there." And he goes in and typical, beautiful firemen that they are—great, great people—he goes right through the flames to the second floor and finds two more of these guys hiding in the dirty laundry and he pulls them down the stairs. Next day they ran an editorial about my rescue of these poor people. The Press Club gave me an award for that, too. I was covering labor at the time. A few days later, two of the firemen, one an assistant chief, came to the city room and asked if they could see Russ Kane. They presented me with a beautiful plaque with a firefighter figure on it. It reads, "To William F. Miller, for your outstanding and meritorious service rendered in assisting the Cleveland Fire Department and your courageous rescue effort on behalf of the victims of the fire on January 17, 1967. Presented by Firefighters Local 93, Cleveland, Ohio." They made me an honorary member of Local 93.

MIKE ROBERTS
*Reporter, Editor,* Plain Dealer

I was in Vietnam about a month and I traveled to Cu Chi, which is about 20 miles outside of Saigon. I was with a civilian advisor and he says to me, "We've got a guy who's an advisor to the district chief." So I walked over and there's Terry Lambacher. I tell him I'm Mike Roberts from the Cleveland *Plain Dealer*. He said, "Shit, I'm from Cleveland."

We start talking and he had just finished a tour with the Special Forces and he went to language school and came back as a civilian advisor. I said, "When you're in town, come to Saigon and come stay with me. I've got a room at the Caravelle anytime you want to come in."

So he would come and the management of the hotel would get pissed because Lambacher would come in with a couple AK-47s, and grenades hanging all over him. This Vietnamese concierge came to me one day and said, "Mr. Roberts. Can we talk? When Mr. Lambacher comes to stay here, he scares the guests."

The Caravelle housed all the visiting diplomats and politicians, and Lambacher was a reminder to them that the war was real.

Lambacher invited me to stay with him at Cu Chi. I got there one night and the Viet Cong attacked his place. I'm mean, it's a firefight like a bitch. I'm in the bunker and he's got a grenade launcher and it's going, "Boom! Boom! Boom! Boom!"

Later I said to him, "Son of a bitch, I'm not going to stay with you anymore, okay?"

Well, the next time I see him he says, "Take a couple of days off. Let's go to Cambodia. Nothing's going happen. We'll have some laughs."

We go to Cambodia on a motorcycle and we pull into a clearing maybe about two clicks into Cambodia. It was a little marketplace. So he starts bullshitting with a Cambodian police chief, who grabs Lambacher and says something to him. I didn't understand the language. What he says to him is, "It would be best if you go now. There are many VC coming."

We got on the motorcycle as groups of men come up to us. One guy is staring at Terry, just a mean fucking stare. It still doesn't dawn on me what is going on. Lambacher, with me behind him, circles the motorcycle around and comes back to these guys in black and gives them the finger before he guns the bike.

Vroom! Now it dawns on me what is happening. We're tearing ass down the road, and I'm waiting for the gunfire.

Later, when I get off the motorcycle, I say, "Never again with you, you son of a bitch. Never, ever again am I going to go anywhere with you." I was so scared I was shaking.

In another one of the attacks on Cu Chi, Lambacher killed a lot of Viet Cong. He had a price on his head. The VC offered a water buffalo to anybody that killed him. He'd go out there and the villagers loved him. That's why he was able to keep alive, because the people would warn him. He'd take the kids out in the rice paddies and they'd throw beer cans up in the air and he'd shoot them with his AK. He'd say, "It's late in the afternoon. The VC will come soon. We've got to get back." And he'd throw grenades into the pond for them to get the fish. Later he won the Vietnamese Medal of Honor for his work at Cu Chi.

WHITEY WATZMAN
*Reporter,* Plain Dealer

I once blundered into a trap that the police had set for an armed robber, a man with a compulsive trigger finger. They had word that he'd made an appointment to see a woman on the second floor of an apartment on East 21st Street, just south of Payne Avenue and the police station. He had blood on his hands, and had been at large for months.

The police arrived more than an hour early in the darkness, with a half dozen men in uniform and plainclothes taking up positions at the top of the stairway, near the front door and in the woman's living room. They brandished shotguns as well as revolvers. They were edgy, fearing for their lives, I guess. They'd been briefed well on the criminal's modus operandi: he would enter darkened buildings, as a precaution, only with his gun drawn. Other policemen had surrounded the building on the outside, but they weren't going to close in until the criminal had entered the front door. A decision had been made to permit him to cross the threshold, climb the stairs and knock on the door of the apartment. Then the police could be sure that they'd have the right man, rather than a visitor to or a tenant in the building.

In the meantime, city editor Jim Collins received a tip that an important police action was about to take place. The informant, choosing to be cryptic, disclosed little more than the address, advising: "Watch that place!"

So I was sent from the police station to watch it.

"Watch for what?" I asked.

"Just be there—that's all," I was told. "Cover what happens."

This is what happened: I saw nothing outside as I arrived on foot, and I didn't know that inside the stage was set for a possible shootout. Uncertain about what else I was supposed to do, I opened the front door. The staircase was in front of me—all was still. I felt uncomfortable in the silence. Had I come too late for something that had already occurred? I decided I ought to check upstairs, so I went up, armed with my nonlethal pencil and notebook, and reached the first landing. I turned 180 degrees and continued upward to the first riser. As my foot came down, sound filled the hallway.

I saw dimly a man coming down the staircase with a shiny object in his hand, pointed at me, and he was swearing at me. I recognized a husky detective I knew from the police station, Sgt. Paul Robinson.

"It's the *Plain Dealer* guy!" he yelled in rage as more men emerged from the darkness. "What the goddamn hell are you doing here?"

"The paper sent me," I said weakly.

"The paper sent him!" he repeated. "Where? To your funeral? You don't belong here! Get your butt out of here! Get going! Get going!"

I retreated, back to the *Plain Dealer* office in the police station. About half an hour later, the criminal was collared—captured alive without resistance—on the same staircase where I'd almost lost my life. Robinson, still angry, told me afterward that his men were determined to shoot first, out of fear that they might not live to use their weapons. They'd decided not to let their quarry open the apartment door because he might have spotted them by the time he got there. They'd held their fire when I arrived, but barely, when Robinson recognized me and signaled them.

They held their fire too when the criminal got there, when they noted that he did not, on this occasion, really have a gun in his hand. It was in his shoulder holster. "I didn't have a gun either," I said to Robinson. "Only a pencil."

"No, but you had something in your hand, and the men were nervous. Do you realize that you and your goddamn paper could have screwed up everything for us? One, we might have drilled the wrong man—you. Two, the crook might have gotten away from us in all the excitement if he'd have come in while you were there. Tell that to your editor because I'm going to report it too. I don't want to ever see you again outside of that damned office of yours!"

So I want to thank publicly my friends at the police force for not killing me that day.

TONY NATALE

*Investigative, General Assignment Reporter,* Press

A story that stands out for me was a bombing—of John Nardi, I think. His car was blown up. He was a Teamster. And I was assigned to get information from the Mob in Little Italy. And I recall driving up there with a black photographer, Van Dillard. We drove up on Mayfield Road, Murray Hill, and we stopped in front of the Italian American Club, where the so-called "Don" was. I forget his name now. It was an Italian guy. This guy was in his early 70s. Anyway, Van said, "I better not go in there with you." And I went in there and I introduced myself. The guy said that he understood why I was there. I didn't take any notes. They said no notes. I said, "OK." So I sat there. And he began to philosophize and give me historical background, nothing at all that had to do with the crime. But it was one of the few times that a reporter had ever gotten an interview with the so-called "Don." And of course, the Mafia later switched from Cleveland to wherever it went. But it was very thrilling. But the paper didn't take any chances of identifying me. I think the *Press* carried the byline "by a *Press* reporter" afterward.

DICK PEERY
*Reporter,* Plain Dealer

About three weeks after I started at the *Call and Post*, I heard after work that there was a shootout and riot in Glenville. I was the only person on darkened Superior Avenue as I drove east from 105th. All of the lights were out. The only illumination was from my headlights and the buildings that were burning along the street. At Lakeview, I got out to take a picture of a squad car engulfed in flames. Then I realized I was framed in the light of the fire and made a perfect target. I got back in my car and continued to the shootout scene. The picture didn't come out anyway. Years later I ran into a secretary who told me that a lot of back shop people at the *Call and Post* thought the new guy was some kind of hero for going out there on his own. Others thought I was a fool. I had thought that was what reporters did to keep from working.

JIM MARINO
*Criminal Courts Reporter,* Press

I remember being scared stiff once because I had just finished covering a trial involving a Euclid judge by the name of Bob Steele, who had an assassin kill his wife. I thought that the two guys who were being tried for her murder were behind bars. I walked into a drugstore to buy a pack of cigarettes and there was one of the guys, Martin Kilbane, standing behind me and he says, "Hello, Mr. Marino."

"What in the hell are you doing out of jail?" I said.

"I'm out on bond pending appeal," he said.

"No hard feelings about the coverage, I hope," I said.

I didn't know right then and there if the guy was going to take me on in the parking lot or what. It scared the hell out of me.

DICK FEAGLER

*Reporter, Columnist,* Press

The first assignment I ever had for the *Press* was a big nursing home fire in a town called Fitchville, which is in the western part of the state. A local paper had already covered it when I got there. Louis Clifford didn't feel we did a good enough job, he wanted more coverage. I think 72 people died or something like that. So I went back and the first place I went was the local paper, the *Register*, and I looked up some old buddies and said, "What do you know? Who did you see?" and all this kind of stuff. I picked their brain and they were nice enough to share their information.

Then we went out and we found out that the insurance companies had beat us there because the insurance companies were very worried about any information given by any personnel in this nursing home. And they're running around telling everybody to shut up. I was with a photographer named Jerry Horton, and we found a big oaf who was the husband of a nurse. And we took him to some bar, which was on an intersection out in the country with a big parking lot around it, and we asked a lot of questions about things. We got some information, so it was pretty good. And then they tracked him down at the bar and told him on the phone that we were out there to screw him and do no good, so he got enraged at us.

We went out and got in the car, and Jerry Horton, who had covered D-day, decided to play a game with the guy. It was like a bullfight. Jerry would run to one end of the parking lot and that guy would charge over there, so by the time he got to the car, Jerry would go to the other end, and he would charge back. So this went on, and finally Jerry had enough of this and he rolled down the window, and Jerry had a tire iron under his seat and he said, "Get away from this car or I'll break your goddamn jaw." Then we drove back and we wrote the story. But I went home that night, and that was the first day. I said to my wife at the time, "You know, I've got to tell you, if every day's like this, I'm not sure I'm going to be able to hack this job."

# 18.

# "We understood each other."

## [ POLITICS ]

*Ah, politics, that comedy of errors from which come some of the best newspaper stories. And why not? The men and women we elect to political office are, sad to say, a reflection of us. We assign to politicians tremendous responsibility, and we give them most of our money. Our marching orders are simple: Make us happy. That's the last simple part of the equation. Perhaps no newspaper beat demands such constant compilation of reliable sources. At the same time, politics writers learn to read and understand the small print in legislation. They stay awake to take notes at finance committee meetings. These reporters have hours like sportswriters; news and information doesn't keep to a 9-to-5 schedule. Political reporters know that the relationship is hardly one-sided; just as political reporters use sources, politicians use reporters. And it is here, in this crowded and frantic arena, that competition between newspapers reaches its highest level.*

**BRENT LARKIN**
*Politics,* Press

The greatest local politician I covered was George Forbes. He was the master of understanding power and the use of power, how to accumulate power. Far better than Ralph Perk. Dennis Kucinich was a very good politician, don't get me wrong. He was elected mayor at age 31, but Dennis was a shooting star. He burned out very quickly as we know, only to reemerge 10 or 12 years later. But Forbes was council president for longer than anyone in the city's history. Forbes is a master at accumulating power and keeping the body in check and being able to—using the carrot and the stick approach with these guys. You have these coups on city council. They threw Forbes out as council president. They announced the coup right after the November of '81 election. Lonnie Burton would replace Forbes as council president. Forbes was in Washington that day. I was one of the people who went out to the airport. I was politics writer at the *Plain Dealer*. He announced to all the TV cameras and everything, "I'm not going to fight it. The council has spoken. They want another leader. I will not lift a finger to overturn what the council has done today."

Then he proceeded to go behind closed doors to pull every lever imaginable to overturn this. He used a young councilman named Mike White as his henchman to attack the black councilmen who had supported the coup. Within 72 hours, the coup had evaporated. George knew exactly the levers of powers to pull. It just fell apart.

DICK FEAGLER

*Reporter, Columnist,* Press

Dennis Kucinich is a piece of work. In my judgment, the problem he has is he's not made to govern. When it comes to running a city, he never had it. I remember going out to one of his ethnic joints—he used to like to eat where you had to wipe the forks first. I wasn't exactly right-wing back then, I was pretty much the other way, and I said, "Dennis, you cannot keep maligning the business community. You just can't keep doing it. You've got to treat your business community like a vein of coal. You've got to form some kind of relationship with them."

I got a call from the "Tom Snyder Show," when he had his late night show on—they wanted me to come out and talk about Kucinich. By that time, he had made waves around the country with various things. So I said, "OK. I'll do that." And I got invited by somebody in Shaker Heights to a going-away party for me to go to the show. I thought it was kind of weird. Now I hardly go anywhere and do anything, but back in those days I used to go—if I got invited someplace, I usually showed up. And what it turned out to be was more or less a pep rally—you go over there and you slam the hell out of Dennis Kucinich. That was the whole point of this thing. I'll tell you what's funny besides that. I get on the plane—they said the expenses were all on the Snyder show. So they send the plane fare or ticket or whatever. So I get on the plane and I fly out to Los Angeles. I get off. There's a limo waiting at the airport. I get in the limo and they take me to whatever hotel I was staying at. I check into the hotel, which is paid for. I come out and go down to the studio. There's the limo driver again. I get in the limo and go down to the studio to do the segment. I was the last one. I was in the suicide seat. I did not malign Dennis. I praised him. The show's over. I get up to go back. I look out on the street and there's nobody there. So I go back in and say to who-ever I can find, "How am I going to get back to the hotel?" They said, "Oh, there's a cab stand about three blocks down." They did all this for you just to deliver your body there. Then after they use your body, hey, walk back to the hotel if you want to. I thought that was very ungracious of them.

BRENT LARKIN

*Politics,* Press

Kucinich was on council for the first six years that I covered city hall. I'd stagger in to work when I was covering city hall sometime between 6:30 and 7. You could count on, invariably, probably on the average of one day a week, you'd come to work in the morning—let's say, quarter till 7—and he's sitting at your desk, waiting for you to get there because he had some idea about something, or something he wanted to say about someone that he knew would generate a story. And in those days, newspapers gave City of Cleveland news a lot more importance than they do today, which is somewhat understandable. Dennis would be at work at least once a week. He'd be sitting there and he'd end up in the newspaper that day. Dennis was very shrewd about using the media.

BRENT LARKIN
*Politics,* Press

Ralph Perk had no business being mayor. He was a decent guy but a bad mayor. He wasn't real smart in terms of bookwise or IQ-wise, but he was street smart. And he was a good politician. But I don't think he was a very good mayor. I covered the entire six years of the Perk administration. Maybe kind of at the end of that period—by the 1977 election, then I was the politics—we called it the "editor" at the *Press,* but I wasn't an editor, I was a reporter. The first election I paid a lot of attention to was in 1971. I really learned a lot during that. I wasn't involved heavily in the coverage, but this was an election where you saw how the nationalities at the time—and up until very recently—had a real impact on politics in Cleveland. You knew about Frank Lausche. But you saw how Perk was able to put himself in a position where he could just use that support he had from the nationalities movement—the Eastern European voting blocs in the city of Cleveland—to become mayor.

BILL TANNER
*Reporter, City Editor,* Press

In the newspaper business you have a sense of government and politics. Not every reporter does, but anybody who wants to

become a main part of the paper has to understand how government works, and you can get that both by reading and by acting,
by going out and covering things, talking to people who are holding office and running for office, and talking to policemen and
prosecutors, all these people that keep the infrastructure going.

DICK FEAGLER
*Reporter, Columnist,* Press

The joke used to be that there was a tunnel from the *Press* to
city hall and Louie Seltzer pulls the strings. And to some degree
that was true. He was the guy, I think, that first got Frank Lausche
interested in running for mayor. He liked Lausche and he liked
Tony Celebrezze, too. Celebrezze came to him and asked, "Do
you think it's too early for an Italian to be mayor of the city of
Cleveland?" I think Seltzer told him it was, but he ran anyway.
When he was campaigning, he always wore the kind of hat that
Fiorello LaGuardia wore. And he would go over to the bar and
campaign in the bar and leave the hat on the bar. He must've
had about 80 of these things. He said, "If you go into a bar and
shake hands, you're only shaking hands with the people in the
bar at the time, but if you leave your hat, the bartender says to
the next group of customers, "Do you see that hat? Do you know
whose that was?"

BRENT LARKIN
*Politics,* Press

I got to know Carl Stokes very well, even though for while we
had a love/hate relationship, on and off again for a long time,
when he decided to come back to Cleveland and leave New York.
This was during the 1980 convention in New York when Feagler
and I had a piece—mostly Feagler—when he gave that story to
us at the convention. He had a ton of charisma, as you know. He
had some big trouble at the end of his life. He had these incidents

with the shoplifting and came back to become a municipal court judge. And this is nothing against being a municipal court judge, but when you think of Carl Stokes, you think of something more than a municipal court judge.

MIKE ROBERTS
*Reporter, Editor,* Plain Dealer

One of the editors wanted to look into areas of conflict of interest and decided that we should start with probate court. "You know, a lot of people die intestate," he said. "They have no relatives around, and they have no will. That money is held by the court and then given to the school system." That's after the court paid lawyers to try to find heirs.

So two of us went in and we collected about five years of records and he wanted us to start locating their relatives. I'm thinking to myself, "How are we going to do that?" Well, we started looking and we came across a file that the library had, that nobody knew about—it was left over from the Depression. It was a make-work project. The death notices were clipped, put on cards with filing tabs and filed alphabetically. Nobody used these things.

There were boxes and boxes of them. And now it's in the mid-'6os. They started that in about 1930. So you had a whole generation of deaths with survivors. If you went to look for Joe Blow, there'd be five or six Joe Blows. But when you'd find the guy you were looking for you located his survivors. We found a number of heirs in one afternoon—I don't remember how many, but it was significant. Then we went to the court and found out that lawyers had been paid thousands of dollars and in some cases had flown to Europe to look for the heirs that they could never locate. We found them right in the basement of the library. The lawyers took the money. That was a good story, and we spent about a year working on it.

BRENT LARKIN
*Politics,* Press

The summer of '71 was when I started, and the mayor was Carl Stokes, who had already announced he wasn't running. Carl Stokes used to have televised news conferences every week. He would put his news conferences on TV for a half hour.

I had been on the beat about a month, and I had done some stories that Frank Gaul had helped me with. He was the councilman who had replaced Jim Stanton on short weighing of meat. This was Bill Tanner's idea. We'd go around to these different stores and buy a bunch of meat and see what it was labeled as weighing. We hired our own professionals to weigh the meat and see if the stores were weighing it accurately. It actually performed a very vital public service. We listed the stores that were cheating the customers, charging them for meat that weighed a lot less than they said. We also published the ones that were doing a good job of it. And we gave the meat to the homeless.

I thought it was a pretty good story. It was my first series of Page One stories. And it reflected very poorly on the Division of Weights and Measures, which was headed by a former councilman.

So I had some question that I was going to nail the mayor of Cleveland on during his news conference. This was the first press conference that I went to of these weekly televised ones. I got up and I asked my question. He turned me inside out. He put me under the fence and started asking me questions that, like an asshole, I thought I could answer. He put me on cross-examination and he just ate me for breakfast. He just made an ass of me on TV. But you learn from that.

JIM NAUGHTON
*Reporter,* Plain Dealer

When I succeeded Todd Simon on the politics beat I had to

compete with Dick Maher, who'd been on the beat for decades for the *Press*. On the first candidate filing deadline, I went to the board of elections office and noticed Dick was standing on the officials' side of the front counter, as if to officially accept the nominating petitions. I was on the public's side of the counter. Dick probably was being magnanimous to the new kid because at one point he looked at me and said, "Would you like to join the Knights of Columbus?" I gave an instinctual reply that was very unfortunate. First of all, it hadn't dawned on me that the K of C was a big deal among Irish pols in Cleveland. And more important, all my life I had heard my father, who was rather cynical, deride the Knights of Columbus, and I repeated to Dick what my dad had claimed he always said in reply to such an invitation: "No, thanks, I already have enough insurance." But I've been lucky all my life, and the exchange was overheard by some pols who thought it was funny or snarky or who had had their fill of Dick Maher, and they kind of adopted me and became great sources.

JOE RICE
*Reporter,* Plain Dealer

Pat Sweeney had a fundraiser and Vern Riffe was there. I went over to Maryann Sharkey, who had written something very caustic. He was reading her the riot act and said, "Why can't you be like Rice?" She and I were walking back to the *PD* and she's shaking. "I can't get over this. You laugh at him. You make jokes about him. You write bad stories. And he still likes you."

I got along good because we understood each other, and that's what it's all about.

JIM NAUGHTON
*Reporter,* Plain Dealer

When I got the politics beat I discovered two things that each scared me. One was that I could write a Sunday review column about local and state politics, which I wound up enjoying and probably spending too much time on. The other was that I was expected to forecast the outcome of the elections on the Sunday before the vote. My first time, I actually thought I should say who I thought would win based on my scanty insight into the process, and a significant majority of my predictions were dead wrong.

There was, at that time, another Cleveland tradition, that the politics writers for the *Press* and *PD* would appear the Friday after the election at the City Club to give their analyses of why things turned out that way. I had become a member of the City Club and knew that many of its members went out of their way to craft the nastiest, most penetrating questions they could conceive for any speaker who dared appear. So I rented a swami turban and a crystal ball from a theatrical supply house that I recall being on Euclid in the theater district. I got one of the *PD* artists to paint a crack on the crystal ball. And then I did a kind of Johnny Carson "Carnac" routine with sealed envelopes bearing questions to which I gave goofy answers, essentially making fun of myself, so I could try to beat the club members to the punch. It worked, was a big hit, and, as I discovered, ate up a bunch of the time for which I would be expected to be intelligent. So I used a similar routine for many years thereafter anytime I got dragooned into making a speech, which I continue to dislike doing.

Someone turned in a photo of me in the Carnac getup and it ran as a *PD* house ad—a full page—prior to a later election. Vail never said a word to me about it but others said he was furious.

# 19.

# "You can't take this away!"

[ THE END OF THE PRESS ]

*The deathwatch started long before June 17, 1982. When it became official, staff members were much like the troops in an army that lost: whatever it was they were fighting for would not be won. In its day, the* Press *was everything a big daily newspaper was supposed to be: vibrant and vigilant, current and controversial, and intimate with its city. For all that, the* Press *found itself in an unenviable position. It came out late in the day and competed with television. When the surrender flag went up, it also signaled a new and lesser age of journalism, one without competition. As if that were any consolation.*

TOM SKOCH

*General Assignment Reporter,* Press

I had always heard stories that the *Press* was in trouble and going to be sold, and I always discounted those because we had heard that over a couple of years. Then I was at my mother-in-law's house and somebody told me, "Hey, the *Press* is sold."

I said, "Ah, come on."

They said, "No, it's on TV."

So I watched the TV newscast and they said the *Press* had been sold to Joe Cole. It just hit me in the gut. All of the sudden I realized, holy cow, it's all true. It's always been true, everything, and it's only a matter of time. This guy doesn't know anything about newspapers. He's a businessman, an industrialist. He's going to get tired of losing money fast. The *Press* was on Ninth and Lakeside, a beautiful piece of property overlooking Lake Erie, on the railroad line. I thought, "Oh, he's going to use that real estate for something else. I've got to get out of here before the ceiling caves in."

And just about that time, the phone rang. It was a job offer from University Hospitals. At the time that the *Press* was sold, I was the medical writer. And the hospital asked me to come over there and do medical writing for them. I ended up going there.

I thought the *Press* would close within five years. And I didn't want to get caught because I had three little kids to feed.

But it only took 18 months. I don't remember the moment I heard the *Press* was closed. My clearest memory was when I heard it was sold because that's when it ended for me. It was closed about 18 months after I left. And then they demolished the building. I remember driving by Lakeside, the building's half down. In the gaping, open wound of a building, I looked up, and the demolition had proceeded right to the spot where I asked my future wife on our first date. When they tore that building down and when it closed, I just felt like my father died. The *Press* was the only place I ever wanted to work. If I was still there as a reporter, I'd be perfectly happy. It was just a great place, like a family of people.

BILL TANNER
*Reporter, City Editor,* Press

The *Press* went under because of all the known reasons—it was an afternoon paper, the competition from other media (television, radio), a little bit of lack of initiative on the part of management to start a Sunday paper.

DON BEAN

*Reporter,* Plain Dealer

When the *Press* and the *Plain Dealer* were competing, I think the *Press* would compete for more local news and the *Plain Dealer* tried to be a *New York Times* of the Midwest. That's one difference, I think. I think the *Press* was more readable, myself, and they had more gung-ho and aggressive reporters, I think. Tom Boardman was a wonderful man, but he didn't do much good for the *Press* when he was appointed editor. I thought it was a bad choice. But it wasn't all his fault. Scripps Howard just didn't pour any money into it. They just let it die for some reason. I was still working when it went under, in '82. I remember when I heard about it. We left the city room at the *Plain Dealer* that morning. We had black armbands and we went down to the *Press* to share their sorrow.

TIM ROGERS

*Sports Reporter,* Press

I was pretty naïve and thought the *Press* would always be around, although from the day I was hired, people asked me, "How long is that paper going to last?" I had no idea what they were talking about. The thought never crossed my mind.

HELEN MOISE

*Food Writer,* Press

The very last day was probably the worst day of everybody's life, even those of us who didn't agree with one another and fought all the time. So we listened to Dorothy Fuldheim and she told us that we were closing. She was on Channel 5 with the news. She had breaking news. Nobody from the paper told us. She told us. So we all gathered around. We saw the door to the office open up and some people coming out, and all the reporters who were still there ran and surrounded the head honchos and we said,

"We understand we're closing tomorrow. Is this true?" They said, "Look, we have a paper to get out tomorrow. So get back to your terminals and get the paper out and then be here at 8 tomorrow. We have a meeting." So we went back to our desks and got the stories out. And then the next day we came in and that's when they told us. To me, it was like losing a parent.

REED HINMAN
*Sports, Suburban Reporter,* Press

The day the *Press* went under I was in the city room. Somebody made an announcement. And we all knew something was going to happen. I can't remember who made the announcement, but there was a picture of everyone huddled around the city desk, and I'm in that picture. Then we had the newspaper to put out that day. I had some function. I can't remember exactly what it was. And we cleaned out our desks and went home. I remember getting home and breaking down crying. It was a very difficult time. My second baby was a year old at that time. A lot of us socialized together, too, and there were some of us who were about the same age and had been married about the same time, and it was a tough one.

HARRIET PETERS
*Television Reporter,* Press

The very worst time was the evening before the final day. I was the one who really made the announcement to the staff, because it was late afternoon. One reporter who I was particularly close to at the time was Susan Howard [from Channel 8, WJW]. She called me and said, "I need you to verify that the *Press* is closing tomorrow." Of course, I didn't know that nor did anybody but the higher-ups.

I let out a scream because I was so shocked. Everybody came running to my desk asking, "What happened?" and I told them and then they all went to tune in the early news. The reports on the news were speculating that we were going to close and so, that night after work, most of us, even people that really didn't drink or didn't socialize that much, we all went over to the Holiday Inn, which was next door to the *Press* building that no longer exists. Even the *Plain Dealer* people, many of them came over and bought us drinks and consoled us. We shared memories, and then the next day at 8:30 A.M.—the official announcement.

BRENT LARKIN

*Politics,* Press

When the *Press* went under, that day, I was here at the *Plain Dealer*. I forgot how I heard about it. I remember we walked over there in solidarity and everybody stood outside. That night I think there was something down at the Headliner. I prefer to remember the days from the early part of the '70s when I was at the *Press*, and the days the others talked about, the glory days. But the last two years, the *Press* wasn't a very good place to work.

TEDDI GIBSON-BIANCHI

*Entertainment Critic, Medical Reporter,* Press

I was reviewing Karamu and it was one of the few times my husband came with me. He didn't usually do that. Karamu was doing an updated version of a Shakespeare play, "The Taming of the Shrew." And at intermission, the PR person said to me, "Gee, I'm really sorry to hear about the *Press*." I'm looking at her, thinking to myself, "Oh, there have been many of these rumors about the paper going under for the last couple of years." And I sort of shrugged it off and didn't think anything more about it.

Back at the office I'm greeted with the SWAT team. They're checking everybody's ID. I asked the chief copy editor, "Should I write this or not?" He said, "Yeah. Go ahead and write it." So I write the review probably the fastest I've ever done it, in, like, 45 minutes. And it was in the last published paper. It was startling. It was surreal, in a way. Instead of being a news reporter, you become a player in a news story, what's going to be a news story for somebody else.

FRANK HRUBY
*Music Critic,* Press

It was 6 o'clock and I was driving and had the evening news on the radio. I was driving down Chester Avenue and I heard, "It seems more than a rumor that tomorrow's edition of the *Press* will be the last one." Joe Cole—I always assumed that he bought the *Press* for some reason, but I couldn't figure out why. He had said words to the effect that "You must have two newspapers in Cleveland, we can't only have one." Within 18 months or so, he sold out. But he had acquired the property that the *Press* owned.

GEORGE VUKMANOVICH
*Copy Boy,* Press

Bill Barrett was the TV columnist. He was out on the West Coast. The TV networks were going to be running their new shows for prime time. So there were a bunch of TV critics and stuff from around the county that came out there and they showed the stuff. And he was out there at the time and we got the notice that the *Press* was folding. The next day would be the last day. This was on a Wednesday. So I got the number of the hotel that Bill was staying at. I called him and he wasn't there. I said, "Can you have him call me at the *Press* immediately? It's absolutely essential. I have to talk to him. It's very important, before he does anything else."

So I got the call from Barrett. He said, "If there's any problem with the copy . . ."

"Bill, don't worry about it," I said. "The story no longer means anything because we're folding tomorrow. That's it."

Well, the upshot of it was, I guess they had canceled the company credit card or something, and he was stuck out on the West Coast. So they had to pass the hat around, chip in and put money in so he could buy his plane fare back to Cleveland.

HARRIET PETERS
*Television Reporter,* Press

After the *Press* folded it took me a while to get a job because unemployment was much higher than it had been in the last few years, it was double digits, unemployment in 1982. When I ended up working at St. Alexis Hospital for community relations, it was such a culture shock. I know when I was telling stories to people at work there, they would just look at me blankly. There was just no understanding. They kept thinking why would anybody want to work in such a setting when they were in their own offices, and sometimes they would close the door. I have no regrets.

TIM ROGERS
*Sports Reporter,* Press

When we walked out, we were checked to make sure we weren't stealing phones or typewriters.

HARRIET PETERS
*Television Reporter,* Press

I had a Royal manual typewriter. We just loved those things. I can remember just hugging it and saying, "You can't take this away!"

# Acknowledgments

Many people have been kind to me. For reasons I still can't fathom, Bill Tanner hired me. I regret I was unable to reward his confidence. Ned Whelan and Mike Roberts encouraged me, Norm Mlachak and Dick Peeples befriended me, Don Bean amazed me. He still does. Dick Feagler took me out for martinis my first night on police beat, thus ensuring rounds were not called. Bill W. and Dr. Bob saved my life. I'll always be grateful to Rich Osborne and Ed Walsh, who, over the years, did two things for me: kept me working and showed me just how good editors can be.

— JHT